**Federal Aviation
Administration**

DOT/FAA/AM-13/12
Office of Aerospace Medicine
Washington, DC 20591

Aviation Medical Examiner 2012 Feedback Survey: Content Analysis of Recommendations

Brenda M. Wenzel
Katrina B. Avers
Joy O. Banks
Civil Aerospace Medical Institute
Federal Aviation Administration
Oklahoma City, OK 73125

June 2013

Final Report

NOTICE

This document is disseminated under the sponsorship of the U.S. Department of Transportation in the interest of information exchange. The United States Government assumes no liability for the contents thereof.

_____

This publication and all Office of Aerospace Medicine technical reports are available in full-text from the Civil Aerospace Medical Institute's publications Web site: www.faa.gov/go/oamtechreports

Technical Report Documentation Page

1. Report No. DOT/FAA/AM-13/12	2. Government Accession No.	3. Recipient's Catalog No.
4. Title and Subtitle Aviation Medical Examiner 2012 Feedback Survey: Content Analysis of Recommendations		5. Report Date June 2013
		6. Performing Organization Code
7. Author(s) Wenzel BM, Avers KB, Banks JO		8. Performing Organization Report No.
9. Performing Organization Name and Address FAA Civil Aerospace Medical Institute P.O. Box 25082 Oklahoma City, OK 73125		10. Work Unit No. (TRAIS)
		11. Contract or Grant No.
12. Sponsoring Agency name and Address Office of Aerospace Medicine Federal Aviation Administration 800 Independence Ave., S.W. Washington, DC 20591		13. Type of Report and Period Covered
		14. Sponsoring Agency Code

15. Supplemental Notes

Work was accomplished under approved task AM-A-08-HRR-521

16. Abstract

The Civil Aerospace Medical Institute (CAMI), as a component of the Office of Aerospace Medicine (OAM), surveyed the population of aviation medical examiners (AMEs), as federal designees, in 2012 to assess their satisfaction with Federal Aviation Administration (FAA) airman medical certification services and to gather their feedback on how to improve those services. Reported here are results from an indepth content analysis of AME recommendations for improving medical certification services, systems/tools, processes, and policies.

One in five AMEs (438 of 2,118: 392 domestic and 46 MFI—military, federal, international) that met the survey selection criteria responded to at least one of the open text items. Of those, most reported being a senior AME (75% domestic, 81% MFI). All domestic and international regions were represented by the respondents. Of note, the majority of those providing recommendations who reported use of a medical certification service in the past 12 months also reported satisfaction with the service.

AME feedback regarding development of organizational services identified needs for: training, real time/anytime access to FAA physicians, specific information, timely communication and specific content in correspondence, speedier FAA decisions, reduced costs, quality interactions with FAA personnel, and an increase in FAA staff. Feedback regarding enhancements to systems/tools included need for: new capabilities, ready and stable access, end user support in effective and efficient task performance, easier to use and read interfaces and printouts, and adjustment to existing capabilities. Feedback regarding changes to medical certification processes and policies addressed requirements for: transmission of reports, records, and documents to the FAA; airmen applications; exam appointments; issuance decisions; printed certificates; and AME rules. Some of the recommended improvements may not be feasible due to operational, financial, or regulatory constraints. Results provide a programmatic view of AME-recommended improvements and can be used to inform future OAM decisions regarding medical certification services.

17. Key Words Content Analysis, Service Quality, Program Evaluation, Aviation Medical Examiner, Airman Medical Certification		18. Distribution Statement Document is available to the public through the Internet: www.faa.gov/go/oamtechreports	
19. Security Classif. (of this report) Unclassified	20. Security Classif. (of this page) Unclassified	21. No. of Pages 44	22. Price

Form DOT F 1700.7 (8-72) Reproduction of completed page authorized

i

ACKNOWLEDGMENTS

Thanks to Janine King, Suzanne Thomas, and Carrie Roberts for support in the development and administration of the survey, and preparation of the database. Your efforts were integral to this research. A special thanks to Mike Wayda and Kathy Wade for your edits and assistance in publishing the report.

CONTENTS

Aviation Medical Examiner 2012 Feedback Survey: Content Analysis of Recommendations

ACRONYM LIST

AASI ----------- AME assisted special issuance
AMCD ---------- Aerospace Medical Certification Division
AMCS ---------- Aerospace Medical Certification Subsystem
AME ----------- aviation medical examiner
AMED ---------- Aerospace Medical Education Division
ANG-C1 -------- FAA NextGen Human Factors Division
AsMA---------- Aerospace Medical Association
BP ------------ blood pressure
CAD ---------- coronary artery disease
CME---------- continuing medical education
CSR ---------- cortisol secretion rate
ECG ---------- electrocardiogram
ETOH -------- ethyl alcohol
FAA ---------- Federal Aviation Administration
FAQ ---------- frequently asked question
FTP ---------- File Transfer Protocol
HIMS-------- Human Intervention Motivation Study
HIPAA ------- Health Insurance Portability and Accountability Act
HTTP -------- Hyper Text Transfer Protocol
IP ------------ Internet Protocol
JNC --------- Joint National Committee
MFI --------- military, federal, and international
MMAC------- Mike Monroney Aeronautical Center
NASA-------- National Aeronautics and Space Administration
OAM -------- Office of Aerospace Medicine
OSA -------- obstructive sleep apnea
SI ----------- special issuance
SSRI -------- selective serotonin reuptake inhibitor
Q&A-------- question and answer
RFS-------- Regional Flight Surgeon
SSN -------- Social Security number
UK --------- United Kingdom
U.S. ------- United States
V&V-------- verification and validation

EXECUTIVE SUMMARY

The Civil Aerospace Medical Institute (CAMI), as a component of the Office of Aerospace Medicine (OAM), surveyed the population of aviation medical examiners (AMEs), as federal designees, in 2012 to assess their satisfaction with Federal Aviation Administration (FAA) airman medical certification services and to gather their feedback on how to improve those services. Needed service improvements identified by survey respondents were captured several ways, including multiple-choice, ranking, and open text items. The format allowed for the collection of a wealth of data in terms of detail and volume.

Reported here are results from an in-depth content analysis of AME recommendations for improving 10 specific medical certification service areas, processes, and policies. Recommendations made by U.S., civilian AMEs were analyzed separately from the military, federal, and international (MFI) AMEs recommendations, not for the purpose of comparison but due to different operational conditions. Results provide a programmatic view of AME-recommended improvements and can be used to inform future OAM decisions regarding medical certification services.

One in five AMEs (438 of 2,118: 392 domestic and 46 MFI) that met the survey selection criteria responded to at least one of the open text items. Of those, most reported being a senior AME (75% domestic, 81% MFI). Half of the domestic respondents reported at least 20 years of experience as an AME and conducting at least 78 exams in the previous 12 months (range 3-3,800). Half of the MFI respondents reported at least 15 years of experience as an AME and conducting at least 30 exams in the 12-month period (range 1-300). All domestic and international regions were represented by the respondents. Of note, the majority of those providing recommendations who had used the medical certification service in the past 12 months reported satisfaction with the service.

Domestic AMEs provided 794 recommendations and the MFI group provided 101. Actionable feedback categories emerged based on common content identified during the initial phases of the content analysis. The feedback categories converged on three main areas for improvement, which were to develop organizational capability, enhance digital systems/tools, and change medical certification processes/policies. Ninety-six percent of the 895 recommendations were classified under one of the main areas, with nearly twice as many recommendations pertaining to development of organizational capabilities, compared to the latter two areas. The 4% of recommendations excluded from the final phase of the content analysis were classified as miscellaneous.

The actionable feedback for the three high-level areas follows in order of priority, i.e., largest to smallest frequency. AME feedback regarding development of organizational capability included need for: training, real time/anytime access to FAA physicians, specific information, timely communication and specific content in correspondence, speedier FAA decisions, reduced costs, quality interactions with FAA personnel, and an increase in FAA staff. Feedback regarding enhancements to systems/tools included need for: new capabilities, ready and stable access, end user support in effective and efficient task performance, easier to use and read interfaces and printouts, and adjustment to existing capabilities. Finally, feedback regarding changes to medical certification processes and policies addressed requirements for: transmission of reports, records, and documents to the FAA; airmen applications; exam appointments; issuance decisions; printed certificates; and AME rules. Some of the recommended improvements may not be feasible due to operational, financial, or regulatory constraints.

Aviation Medical Examiner (AME) 2012 Feedback Survey: Content Analysis of Recommendations

1.0 INTRODUCTION

The Civil Aerospace Medical Institute (CAMI), as a component of the Office of Aerospace Medicine (OAM), periodically surveys the population of Aviation Medical Examiners (AME) to assess their satisfaction with airman medical certification services and to gather their feedback on how to improve those services. Survey respondents provide feedback via multiple types of items, to include open text. Reported here are the analytic approach and results from an in-depth content analysis[1] conducted on the open text recommendations for improving agencies' services, digital systems/tools, training, and certification processes and policies. The results provide a programmatic view of AME-identified improvements and frame results in actionable terms.

Background on the AME survey is provided in this section. Details of the content analysis procedure and results follow, respectively, in Sections 2.0 and 3.0. A discussion of the results is presented in Section 4.0.

overall satisfaction of AMEs with services and quality aspects of services provided by OAM components [i.e., Aerospace Medical Education Division (AMED), Aerospace Medical Certification Division (AMCD), and Office of the Regional Flight Surgeon (RFS)] that they may request or receive support from. The survey also captured AME feedback on improvements to offered services, training, the deferral process, standards and guidelines for medical certification, and tools (i.e., digital electrocardiogram (ECG) system, Internet-based Aerospace Medical Certification Subsystem (AMCS), MedXPress, and OAM website[2]). Survey items on training covered a 3-year period; all other items covered a 12-month period, with the exception of the demographic items.

1.4 Survey Structure and Item Types

The survey design allowed an AME to skip irrelevant items. For instance, if an AME reported no interactions with an agency in the past 12 months, then no additional satisfaction or feedback data on the agency were collected. Thus, the number of

Table 1. Service providers and services presented for open text recommendations

1. AMED	7. Digital ECG System
2. AME Training	8. AMCS Internet System
3. AMCD	9. MedXPress
4. RFS Office	10. Online Information and Publications
5. Deferral Process	11. Other Recommendations
6. Standards and Guidelines	

1.1 Purpose of the Survey

Survey results are used by the OAM to improve services provided to AMEs. Administration of the survey meets federal requirements set forth initially by Executive Order No. 12862, "Setting Customer Service Standards," and the Government Performance and Results Act of 1993.

1.2 Selection Criteria for Survey Respondents

In 2012, the survey was administered to all active AMEs—domestic, military, federal, and international. An invitation to participate from OAM was sent to 3,393 AMEs. However, only data from respondents who report having served as a designee for at least a year and examined at least one airman applicant for certification within the previous 12 months were included in the content analysis.

1.3 Survey Content

The survey items were developed to provide both general and specific feedback to the OAM. Survey items measured the

items presented to an AME depended on that AME's exposure to different agencies over the evaluation period. Those who met the selection criteria (described next) had the option to respond to at least 41 of 107 possible items.

The survey was made up of various types of items—single-choice (e.g., yes/no, satisfaction rating scales, demographic categories), ranking (e.g., indicate top 3), mark all that apply (e.g., reasons why and needed improvements), numeric write-ins (e.g., percentages, number of years) and open text (e.g., explanation of "other," recommendations). The final survey item asked for additional recommendations, beyond what was already provided in the ranking questions, on improving airman medical certification services (Table 1).

2.0 Analytic Approach

A phased-approach was used in the content analysis. The overarching goal was to convert the qualitative data collected with the open text items into quantitative data by coding it into meaningful actionable feedback categories relevant to the AME program goals. With that, the following phases were conducted: (1) preparation of the datasets and conduct of an independent

---

[1] Content analysis is a data reduction technique used to systematically and objectively extract meaning of text entries, thereby converting qualitative data into quantifiable terms (see U.S. General Accounting Office, 1996).

[2] http://www.faa.gov/about/office_org/headquarters_offices/avs/offices/aam/

Table 2. Counts for domestic respondents, and coded responses and comments

	AMED	AME Training	AMCD	RFS Office	Deferral Process	Standards & Guidelines	ECG System	AMCS	Med-XPress	Online Info & Pubs	Other
Respondent	16	91	39	69	49	73	53	62	110	39	103
Coded Response	18	125	64	70	31	60	62	67	69	57	171
Coded Comment	4	18	7	41	6	6	9	12	39	17	21

verification and validation (V&V) of the data; (2) identification of coding categories and development of coding protocols, code book, and data collection sheets; (3) familiarization of multiple raters with the data collection sheets, coding protocol, and use of the code book; (4) execution of the coding protocols by the trained raters; (5) calculation of interrater reliability scores and comparison of the average scores to the 70% criterion (Stemler, 2004); (6) creation of actionable feedback categories by partitioning coded responses based on common content/themes identified during phase 2; (7) calculation of category frequencies and presentation of detailed results.

2.1 Data Review and Preparation

The first phase of the content analysis involved sifting through the open text responses to the 11 items. This was done for purposes of (a) becoming familiar with the various classes or themes present to inform the coding protocol, and (b) identifying codable units[3] to ensure all raters coded the same text.

A recommendation was defined as a response that either stated a needed improvement outright or stated an issue or problem that needs resolution (or both). There was no limit on the number of recommendations from a single AME.

Response content that was irrelevant to the service area it was entered under was partitioned for later review by a näive rater tasked with conducting the V&V, prior to distributing the dataset to the raters.

2.2 Development of the Coding Protocol

A coding protocol was developed to capture the breadth of content provided by AMEs. The coding protocol was provided to the raters as part of a code book, which contained tabled classification codes, along with example wording for each of the service areas and "other recommendations."

2.3 Raters and Interrater Reliability

Three raters were used to conduct the content analysis. The lead rater trained each rater on how to use the coding protocols and datasheets. The lead rater coded all responses. The other raters independently coded a minimum of 10% of the item responses. A consensus-based interrater reliability estimate, calculated as percent of times raters are in agreement, was used to assess consistency in applying the coding protocol (Stemler, 2004; see also Graham, Milanowski, & Miller, 2012). Interrater reliability estimates were computed and averaged for all pairs of raters across the 11 open text items.[4] The average overall reliability score of 83% surpassed the established criterion of 70%, which was required to move to the next phase of the content analysis.

2.4 Actionable Feedback

Common content/themes of all coded recommendations served as the basis for the actionable feedback categories. Descriptions of the actionable feedback associated with each high-level category are presented in the next section. In the process of partitioning the recommendations, three high-level categories emerged that framed results in programmatic terms: (a) development of organizational capabilities, (b) enhancements to systems/tools, and (c) changes to processes and policies.

3.0 RESULTS

Results are reported by type of AME, not for purposes of comparison, but due to different operational conditions. Two AME groups were created--a domestic group and a combined military, federal, and international (MFI) group. Descriptive statistics[5] used in the analysis included: frequency (count), percent (as valid percent, based on actual number of responses to a survey item), range (minimum to maximum value), average [mean and median (med) (50th percentile)], and standard deviation (sd).

Of the 3,388 AMEs invited to participate, 2,199 submitted a survey, and 2,118 met the selection criteria[6] for inclusion of their data.[7] The vast majority of AME respondents (98.2%) submitted their responses online either from a computer or mobile device. The remaining 1.8% returned a paper version of the survey, which they had requested and received in the mail.

3.1 Respondents and Open Text Response Totals

Approximately one in five (438 of 2,118) of the AMEs provided a response to the final text-entry item asking for "additional recommendations, beyond those you have already provided, on how the FAA can improve airman medical certification support and services." Of the 1,840 domestic AME respondents, 392 (21.3%) provided at least one response. As for the 278 MFI AME respondents, 46 (16.5%) provided at least one response.

---

[3] A codable unit refers to a single distinct improvement/issue that is meaningful to the survey question. Of note, a single sentence may contain more than one codable unit, and multiple sentences may constitute a single codable unit.

[4] Raters were provided refined definitions of the coding categories in conjunction with follow-on training before being tasked with independently coding an additional 10% of responses for those service areas with consensus estimates below criterion.

[5] Inferential statistics conducted for exploratory purposes are not reported.

[6] Selection criteria were a minimum of 1 year as an AME and in the previous 12 months had examined at least 1 airman applicant.

[7] See Civil Aerospace Medical Institute (2012a, 2012b).

Table 3. Counts for MFI respondents, and coded responses and comments

	AMED	AME Training	AMCD	RFS Office	Deferral Process	Standards & Guidelines	ECG System	AMCS	Med-XPress	Online Info & Pubs	Other Areas
Respondent	3	12	5	5	7	3	9	18	11	5	10
Coded Response	4	19	4	8	8	1	9	18	3	5	22
Coded Comment	0	5	1	1	0	0	1	5	4	0	0

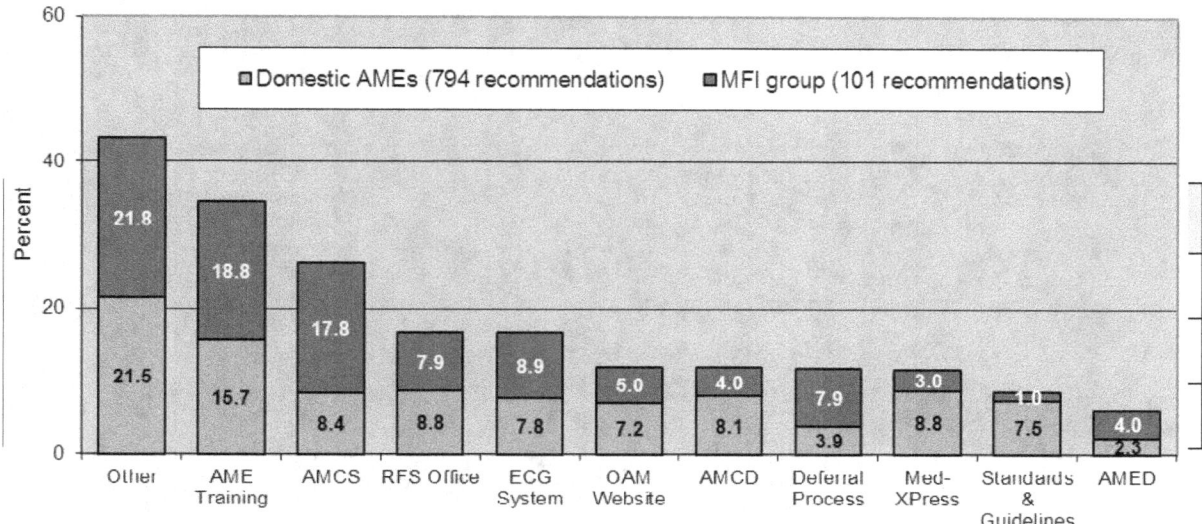

Figure 1. Overview of coded responses across service areas and "other"

Responses that met the definition of a recommendation--*a needed improvement stated outright or an issue/problem that needs addressing*--were deemed codable. In total, 895 recommendations were received. Domestic AMEs provided 794 codable responses, and the MFI group provided 101. One hundred and ninety-seven responses did not meet the definition and were analyzed separately as comments. Tables 2 and 3 present breakouts by AME group of respondents, and coded responses and comments across the 11 areas. *Coded* means the content of the text represented a single recommendation or comment. A single respondent could provide multiple recommendations/ comments for any of the service areas and "Other," which was comprised of recommended changes to medical certification processes and policies.

The distribution of coded responses in Figure 1 shows the origin of the data that fed the final phases of the content analysis. The subset of recommendations used in the programmatic analysis is described in subsection 3.3.

Characteristic of the AMEs that provided recommendations are presented next. Although all responses that met the definition of a recommendation were treated as valid perceptions, the demographics of the respondents are important for interpreting and prioritizing feedback.

3.2 Profile of the AMEs That Provided an Open Text Response

The qualifications of those providing recommendations are, in part, reflected in years of experience as an AME, number of airmen examined in a 12-month period, and estimated proportion of practice dedicated to aviation medicine. A gauge of the representativeness of AMEs providing recommendations can be found in relative comparisons of the proportions of the 438 respondents providing recommendations to those who did not and to all AMEs on the survey distribution list.[8]

3.2.1 Qualifications

Demographics for the two AME groups are presented together in Figure 2 but not for comparative purposes. Rather, they are presented together to provide a frame of reference for the experiences that formed the basis of their recommendations. Descriptive statistics for some of the numeric-entry items are presented in Table 4.

---

[8]The distribution list was obtained from the AME Information System (AMEIS).

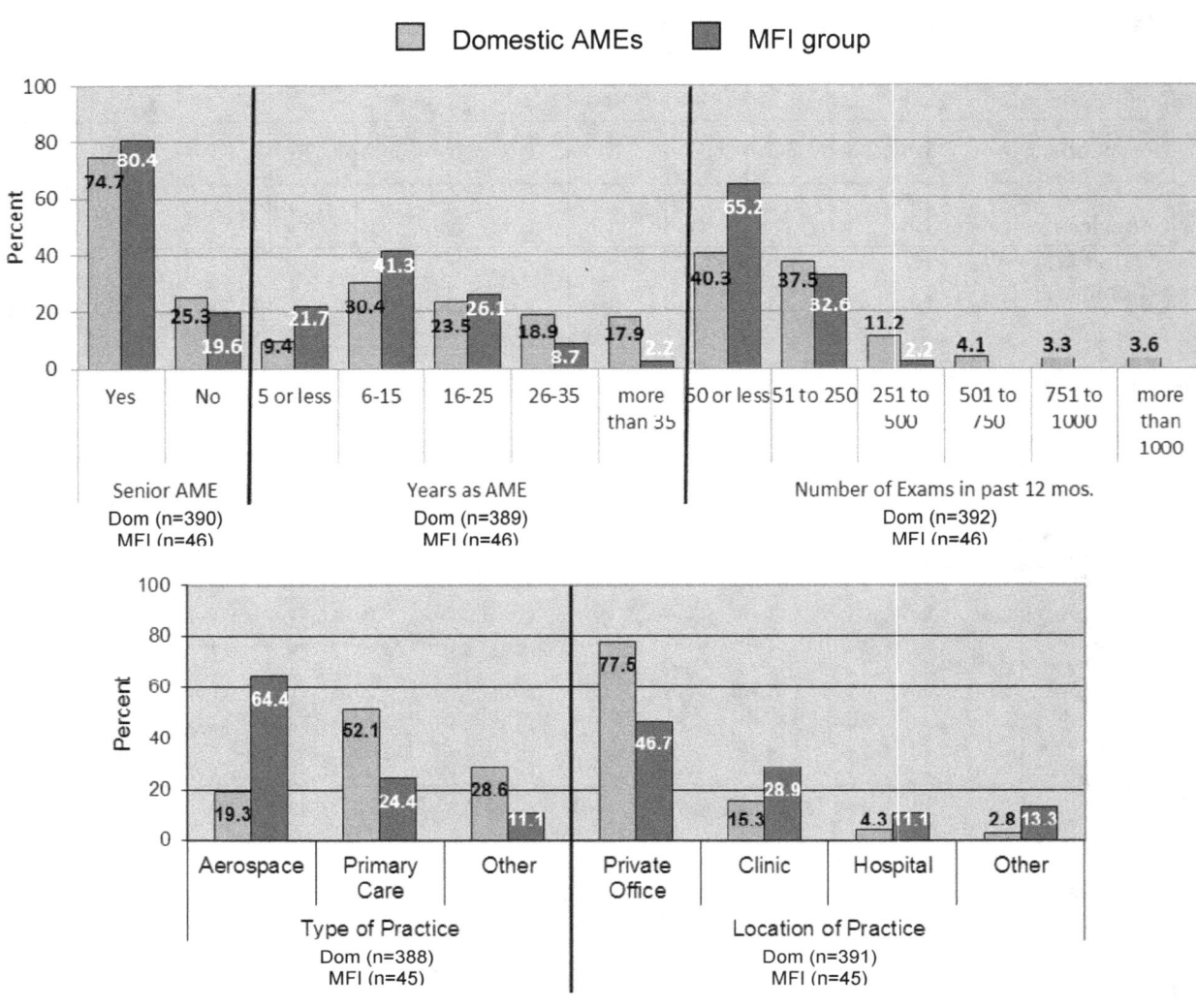

Figure 2. Demographics of AMEs providing a response

Table 4. Descriptive statistics for demographic numeric entry items

Domestic AMEs	mean	sd	range	median
Years as AME (n=389)	22.4	13.2	1-60	20
Number of airman exams conducted in 12-month period	221	391.1	3-3800	78
Percent of practice AME-related	25	34.3	0-100	8
MFI group	mean	sd	range	median
Years as AME	14.6	10.0	1-53	15
Number of airman exams conducted in 12-month period	56	58.9	1-300	30
Percent of practice AME-related	43	35.7	0-100	30

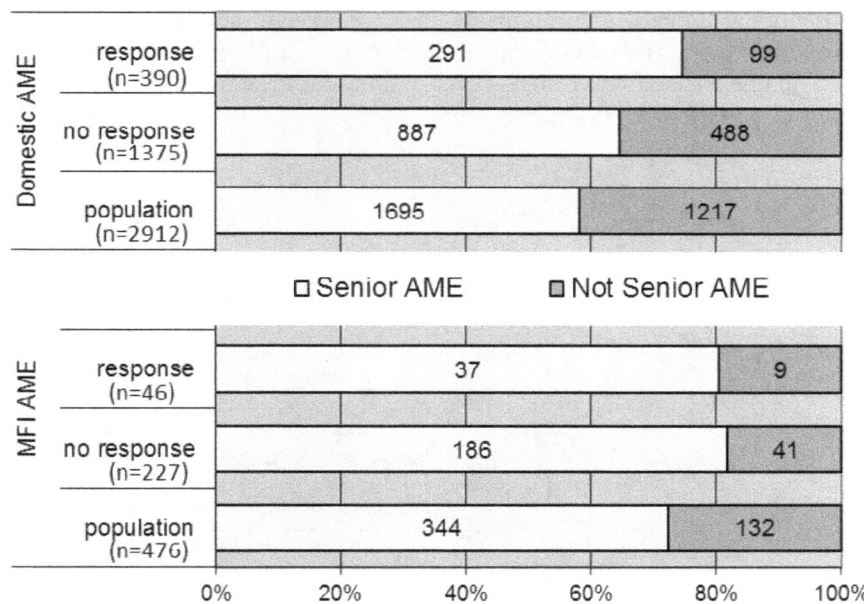

Figure 3. Comparison of the proportions (with count) of AMEs that did and did not provide an open text response to their respective populations

On average, the domestic group tended to have more years of experience as an AME and have examined more airman applicants in the 12-month period than the MFI group. However, more of the MFI group characterized their practices as aerospace medicine, while more of the domestic group characterized theirs as primary care. Patterns were somewhat similar for their practice locations—more reported working out of private offices than elsewhere.

3.2.2 Representativeness

More senior AMEs than AMEs in general provided recommendations on improving services, which would be expected given the higher rate of senior AMEs in the AME population (Fig 3). However, there was a disproportionate number of senior AME to AME that provided recommendations relative to the group population.[9]

With that in mind, response patterns indicated more domestic senior AMEs tended to provide recommendations than not. Senior AMEs from the MFI group did not show the same tendency. With more senior AMEs providing recommendations for improvements, the issues they raised may not fully reflect issues challenging AMEs in general; however, the improvements and changes they proposed would benefit all AMEs at some point in their tenure as designees.

---

[9]The AMEIS dataset used in the survey effort was downloaded March 2012 and the survey closed 31 May. The data's shelf-life may account for discrepancies between the population and survey data, since AMEIS is updated as new information becomes available.

The regional distribution of the domestic AMEs providing an open text response was fairly representative of all domestic AMEs (Fig 4). Note that the Southwest and Great Lakes regions were slightly under-represented, and the Western Pacific region was over-represented.

Although the MFI regional distribution is not delineated to maintain respondent's anonymity, respondents represented all but four regions.

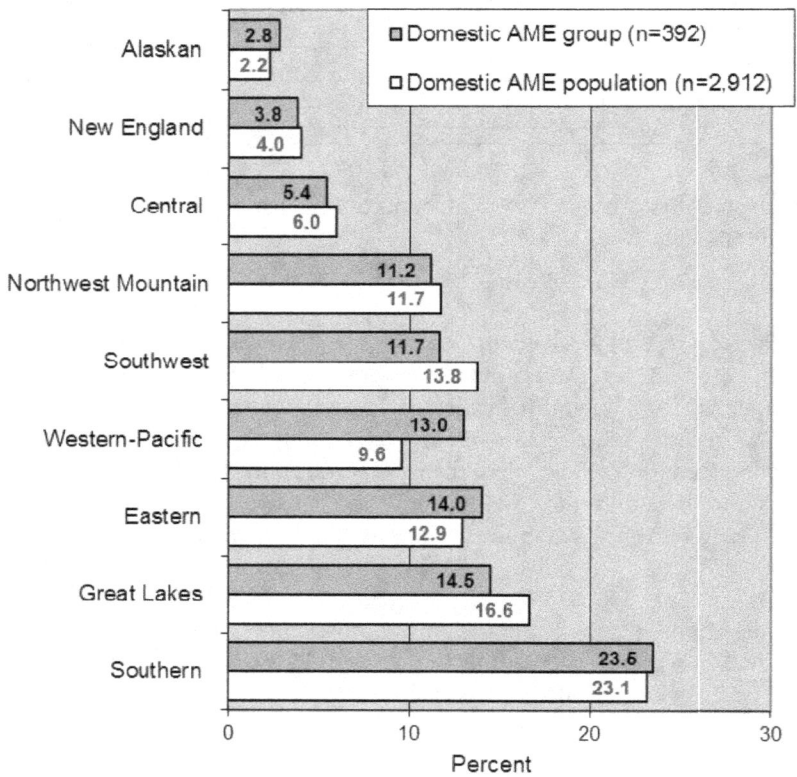

Figure 4. Regional distribution of domestic respondents relative to their population

3.2.3 Satisfaction With Aerospace Medical Certification Services

An examination of AME satisfaction with certification service providers and tools they had used in the past 12 months and agreement with standards and guidelines for deferral was made between those who provided at least one open text response and those who chose not to respond (Table 5). Overall, slightly greater proportions of domestic AMEs responding to an open text item tended to report <u>not</u> being satisfied, compared to those choosing not to respond. The reverse was found with the MFI group for half the service areas rated.

Table 5. Comparison of AMEs NOT satisfied* with airman medical certification services that did and did not provide an open text response

Domestic AMEs					
	response		no response		% difference^
	%	n	%	n	
AMED	15.2	329	10.6	1485	5.4
AMCD	16.5	315	9.3	1089	7.2
RFS	15.7	324	11.0	1157	4.7
AMCS	16.9	388	10.3	1277	6.6
MedXPress	20.6	340	15.0	1176	5.6
ECG System	27.2	250	21.6	745	5.6
OAM Website	21.7	166	15.2	426	6.5
Standards & Guidelines for deferrals are medically reasonable and appropriate	26.3	388	19.3	1385	7.0
MFI Group					
	response		no response		% difference^
	%	n	%	n	
AMED	13.2	38	13.9	187	-0.7
AMCD	19.4	31	18.4	136	-1.0
RFS	33.3	18	16.7	72	16.6
AMCS	20.5	44	19.3	223	1.2
MedXPress	17.2	29	10.7	140	6.5
ECG System	5.3	1	5.6	18	-0.3
OAM Website	5.0	20	13.0	69	-8.0
Standards & Guidelines for deferrals are medically reasonable and appropriate	13.1	38	10.2	196	2.9

*NOT satisfied was calculated as the sum of the percentages of AMEs selecting *Neither*, *Dissatisfied*, and *Very dissatisfied*.

^%Difference was calculated as %*response* minus %*no response*.

Table 6. Comparison of reported use of services* in the past 12 months by AMEs (count) that did and did not provide an open text response

	AMED	AME Training	AMCD	RFS Office	ECG System	AMCS	Med-XPress	OAM Website
Domestic AMEs (n=392)								
Used	15	91	34	61	41	58	93	35
Did not	1	0	5	8	12	4	17	4
MFI Group (n=46)								
Used	3	12	5	5	1	18	8	4
Did not	0	0	0	0	8	0	3	1

*No comparable survey items regarding use of deferrals or standards & guidelines.

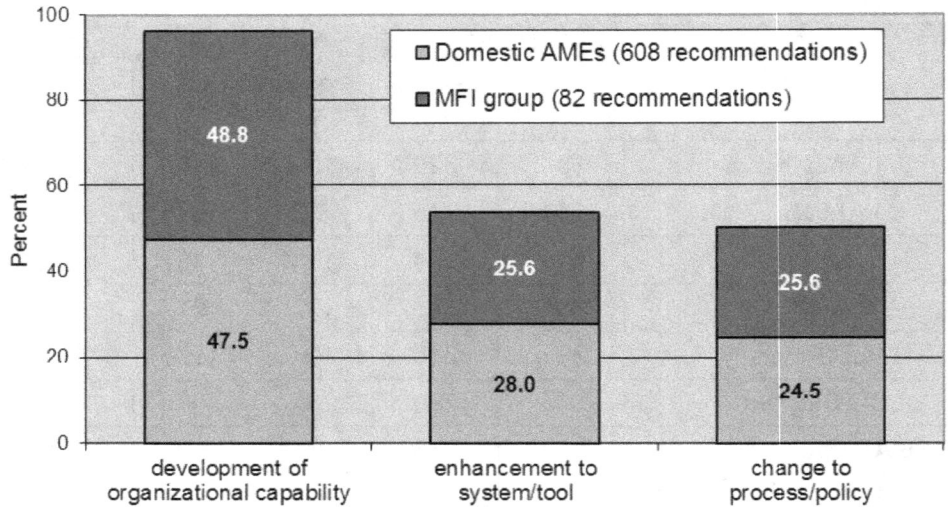

Figure 5. Distribution of AME recommendations across the high-level categories

Satisfaction ratings were collected only if the respondent reported use of the service within the past 12 months. There was no such restriction on the open text items. Shown in Table 6 are the numbers of AMEs providing an open text response to a particular service area based on whether or not the service had been used in the past 12 months.

3.3 Analysis of Recommended Improvements in Actionable Terms

Ninety-six percent (861 of 895)[10] of the coded responses were used in the final phases of the content analysis. Of those, 80% (691) were directly related to the high-level categories. The remaining 170 recommendations were indirectly related to the higher categories and pertained to AME training (94), Standards & Guidelines (52), class of certification requirements (18), and deferral tracking (6).

Figure 5 shows a similar pattern between groups in the distribution of recommendations across the high-level categories.

Results are presented in actionable terms for each of the high-level categories in the following sections: 3.3.1 *Development of organizational capability*, 3.3.2 *Enhancements to digital systems/tools*, and 3.3.3 *Changes to process and policy*.

---

[10]Recommendations excluded from the in-depth analysis were those coded as "miscellaneous."

Table 7. Distribution (percent) of recommendations across service providers

	OAM	AMCD	RFS	AMED
Domestic AME (290 recommendations)	16.6	42.6	22.5	18.3
MFI group (40 recommendations)	15.0	40.0	20.0	25.0

Table 8. Actionable feedback categories for developing organizational capability

Communication (timely, content)	- timeliness of returned phone calls from FAA physicians - content of communication
Cost	- reduce travel expenses for training - reduce cost of equipment/transmission requirements
FAA accessibility (real time/anytime)	- contact with FAA physician while airman in office - access to FAA physician during off hours
FAA decision	- streamline process to shorten decision time - consistency
FAA personnel (interactions, number)	- FAA personnel need to be of service - treat AME professionally with courtesy/respect - more staff
Information request	- FAA personnel contact information - online access to specific content - notification of updates, publications, retraining
Training need	- lack sufficient coverage of content in AME training - gaps in airman education - qualifications lacking in FAA personnel

3.3.1 Development of Organizational Capability

The analysis examined a subset of 330 recommendations[11] compiled from the following sources: AMED (includes AME training), RFS offices, AMCD (includes AMCS and the deferral process), and OAM (includes standards & guidelines, MedXPress, and online information and publications). The pattern of results shown in Table 7 likely reflects the frequency of AME contact across the service providers, with AMCD having the most contact with the respondents. The percentage of recommendations for the service providers was relatively similar between the groups, with the exception of the AMED. The distinct difference in the percentages of recommendations for AMED is due to the MFI group proportionally identifying more AME training needs than the domestic AMEs.

The actionable feedback categories, defined in Table 8, are pertinent to AMEs effectively and efficiently performing their responsibilities as FAA designees. The categories are the common themes that emerged during the coding phase of the content analysis.

---

[11] As a reminder, a valid recommendation either stated how to improve current services or identified a current problem with adequacy of, consistency in, and delivery of services.

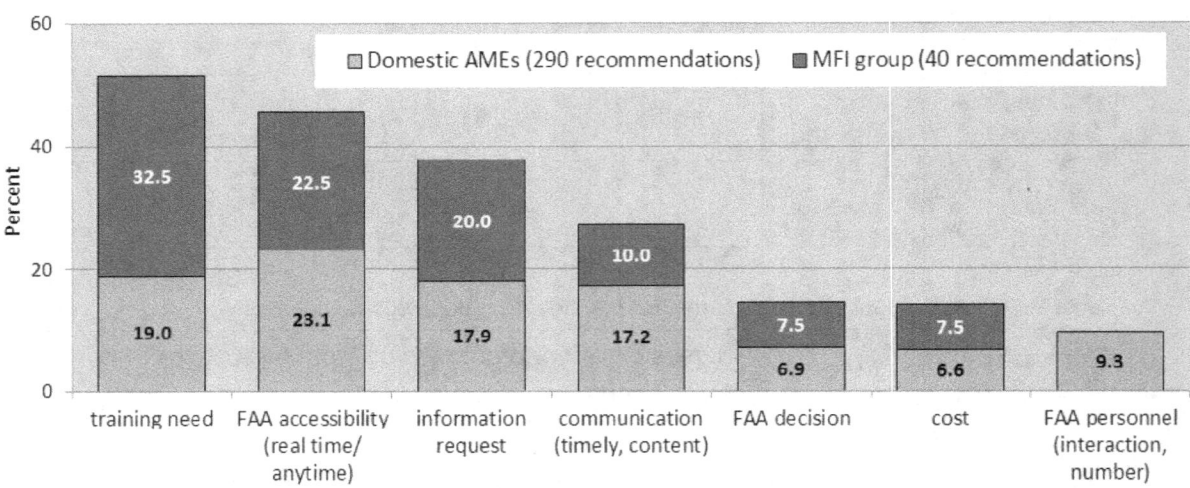

Figure 6. Distribution of feedback for development of organizational capability

Table 9. Training needs (count) from domestic AMEs

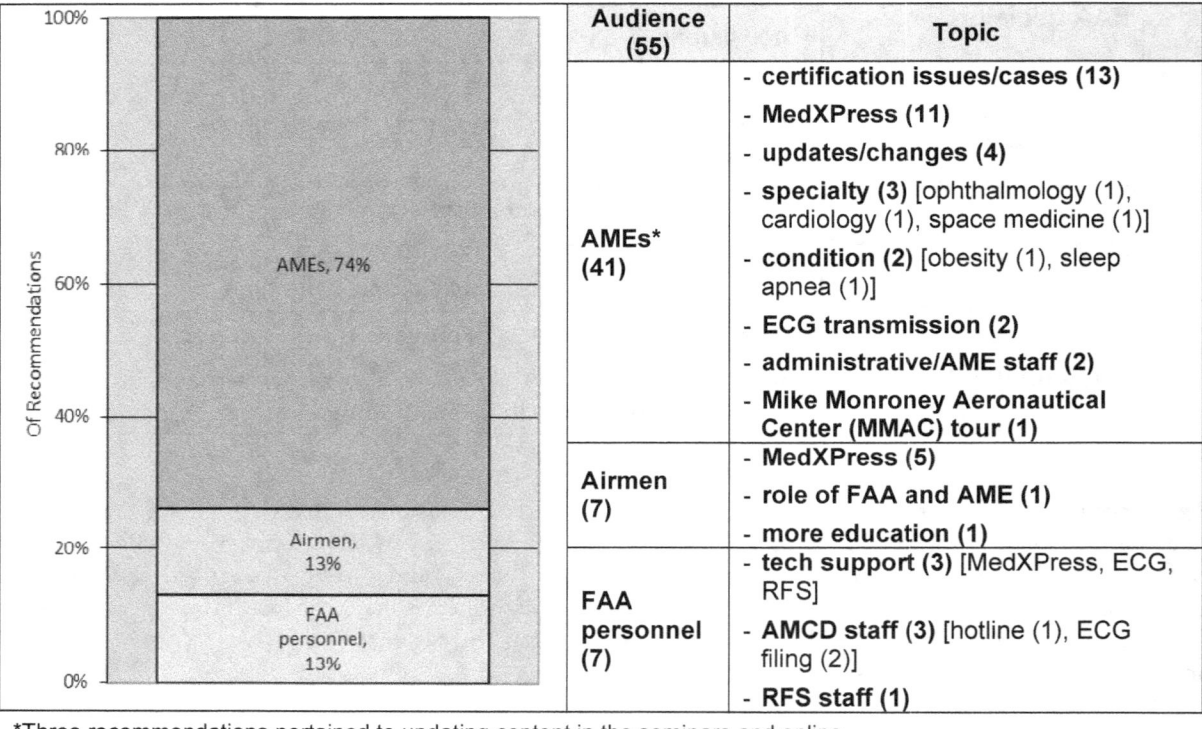

Audience (55)	Topic
AMEs* (41)	- **certification issues/cases (13)**
	- **MedXPress (11)**
	- **updates/changes (4)**
	- **specialty (3)** [ophthalmology (1), cardiology (1), space medicine (1)]
	- **condition (2)** [obesity (1), sleep apnea (1)]
	- **ECG transmission (2)**
	- **administrative/AME staff (2)**
	- **Mike Monroney Aeronautical Center (MMAC) tour (1)**
Airmen (7)	- **MedXPress (5)**
	- **role of FAA and AME (1)**
	- **more education (1)**
FAA personnel (7)	- **tech support (3)** [MedXPress, ECG, RFS]
	- **AMCD staff (3)** [hotline (1), ECG filing (2)]
	- **RFS staff (1)**

*Three recommendations pertained to updating content in the seminars and online.

The distribution of recommendations across the categories (Fig 6) is sorted highest to lowest cumulative percent. Detailed results follow in that order.

The next phase of the analysis involved assigning secondary categories and computing their frequencies. Detailed results for each feedback category are presented next in the tabled format described above by group when they offered five or more recommendations. With the exception of the "training need" and "costs" categories, the results are presented by agency based on origin of the response.

Training Needs. Specified training topics for AMEs, identified need for airman education, and deficits in FAA personnel performance are found in Tables 9 and 10. Most recommendations from domestic AMEs indicated an interest in furthering their understanding of certification requirements for the range of medical issues they may face. Half (7 of 13) of their requests for more training on certification issues indicated a preference for use of case studies. The domestic group also indicated a gap in their and airmen's understanding and use of MedXPress, with an emphasis on addressing it in the near-term. The MFI group referred to the same training needs, in addition to training on AMCS use and ECG transmission.

Table 10. Training needs (count) from the MFI group

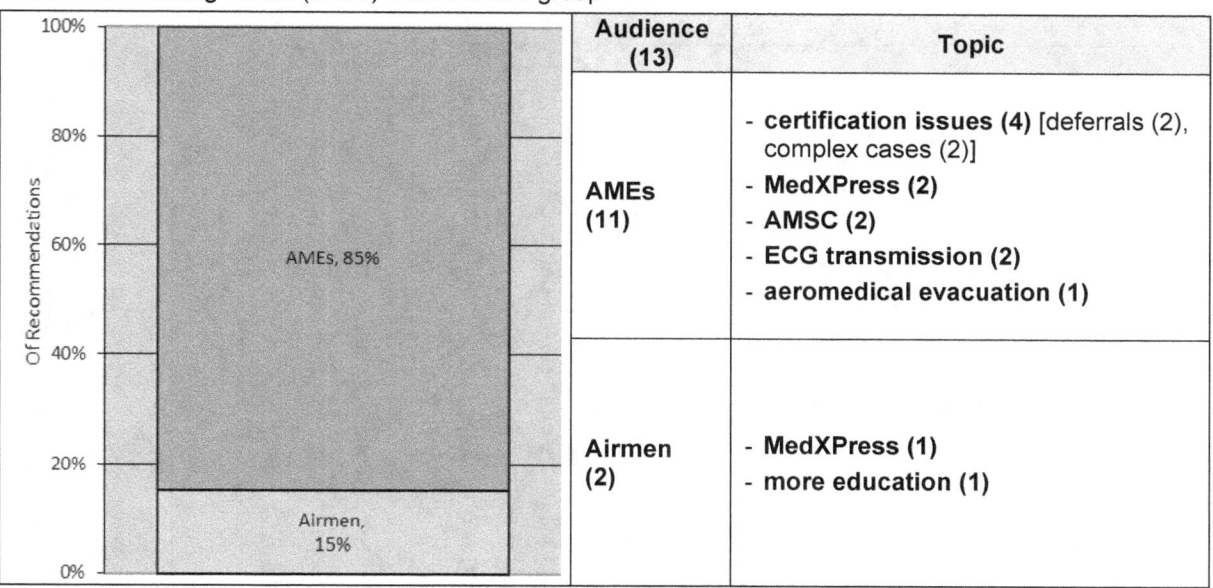

Audience (13)	Topic
AMEs (11)	- **certification issues (4)** [deferrals (2), complex cases (2)] - **MedXPress (2)** - **AMSC (2)** - **ECG transmission (2)** - **aeromedical evacuation (1)**
Airmen (2)	- **MedXPress (1)** - **more education (1)**

AME Training. AMEs identified needed improvements to their training beyond the specific topics reported above. Both groups provided training recommendations on frequency of offerings, strategies (methods and media), locations, and ways to add value that would offset the cost. Table 11 presents results for both AME groups.

Table 11. Distribution of additional recommended improvements (count=94) to AME training

Domestic AME (82 recommendations)

Percent of Recommendations (bar chart):
- location: 25.6
- offering: 25.6
- provide online: 18.3
- method: 12.2
- add value: 12.2
- reduce requirements: 6.1

MFI group (12 recommendations)

Percent of Recommendations (bar chart):
- location: 33.3
- offering: 25.0
- method: 25.0
- add value: 16.7

Domestic AME (82 recommendations)

location (21) [regional (6); tourist site (6); closer to home (5); specified (4: MMAC, NASA, Chattanooga, AsMA)]

offering (21) [more (10); annually (5); monthly (3); not (3: during the week, mid-day, between the 25th and the 3rd; regularly (1); evening of weekend course (1)]

provide online (15) [more options (9); in place of seminars (3); senior AME training (1); refresher training (1); videos of seminars (1)]

training method (10) [small group discussion (3); demonstration (2); experienced "generalists" speakers (2); hands-on (1); problem-solving/Q&A (1); short course (1)]

add value (10) [expand CME activities (6: online courses (4), HIMS, more); testing (3: include specialty topics, require 50 multiple-choice refresher test; instruct to take notes]

reduce requirements (5) [delay retraining (4: longer, every 5-6 years, refresher 1-2 years, skip 7-year fly-in), make performance-based requirement (1)]

MFI group (12 recommendations)

location (4) [regional (2); specified (2: MMAC, UK)]

offering (3) [more often (2), on-demand (1)]

training method (3) [experienced local speakers (2), practice case-studies (1)]

add value (2) CME activities

AsMA=Aerospace Medical Association; CME=continuing medical education; HIMS=Human Intervention Motivation Study; NASA=National Aeronautics and Space Administration; Q&A=question and answer; UK=United Kingdom

12

FAA Accessibility (real time/anytime). A recurrent needed improvement is to provide more access to FAA physicians at the RFS offices and AMCD. The need stems from questions that arise during the applicant's appointment that negatively impacts effectiveness and efficiency of the certification procedure if the AME is unable to contact the FAA. A related challenge for AMEs is the need for information that only an FAA physician can provide when the FAA offices are closed. Several solutions to anytime access were proposed--specifics are presented in Tables 12 and 13. (Note that responsiveness of FAA personnel to AME voice- and e-mail is a component of the "communications" category.)

Table 12. FAA accessibility issues/solutions (count) from domestic AMEs

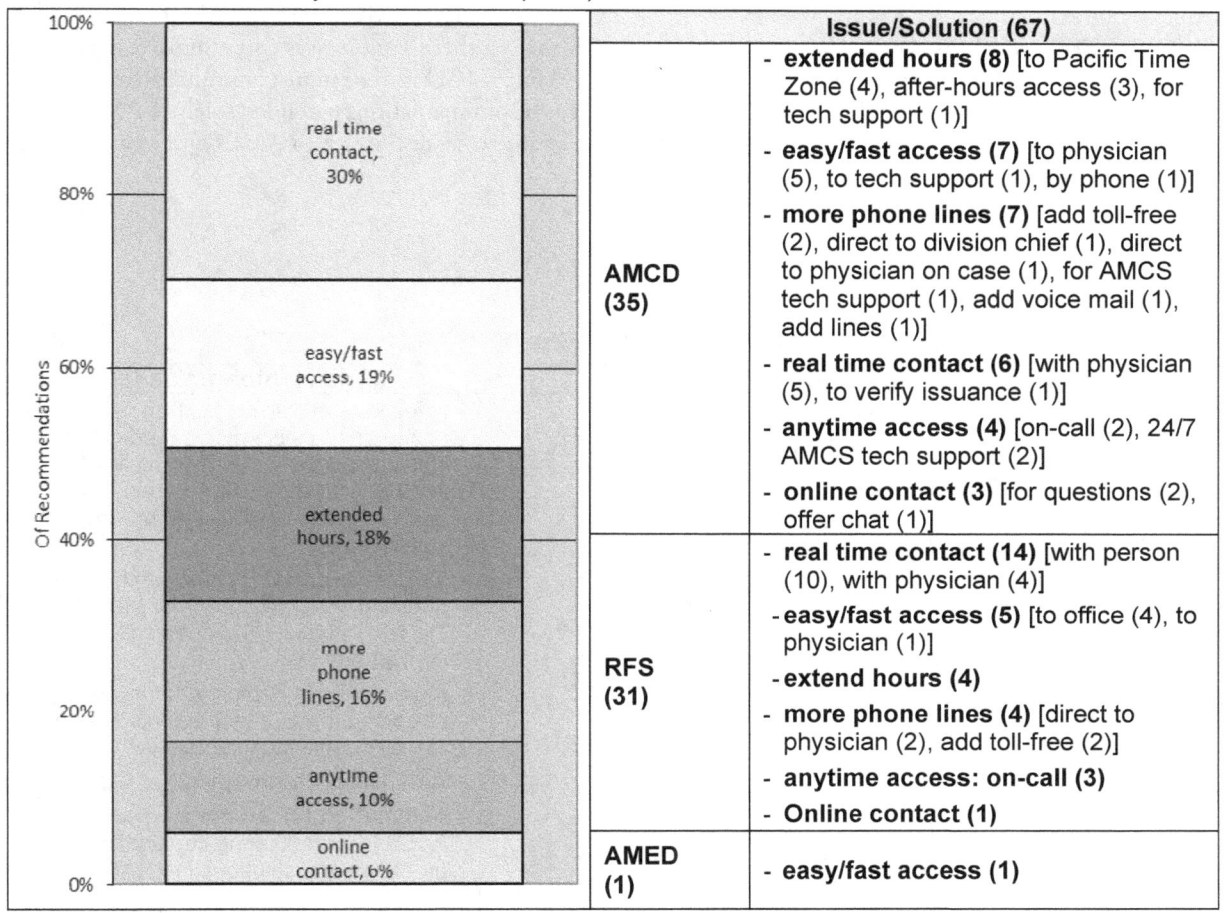

	Issue/Solution (67)
AMCD (35)	- **extended hours (8)** [to Pacific Time Zone (4), after-hours access (3), for tech support (1)] - **easy/fast access (7)** [to physician (5), to tech support (1), by phone (1)] - **more phone lines (7)** [add toll-free (2), direct to division chief (1), direct to physician on case (1), for AMCS tech support (1), add voice mail (1), add lines (1)] - **real time contact (6)** [with physician (5), to verify issuance (1)] - **anytime access (4)** [on-call (2), 24/7 AMCS tech support (2)] - **online contact (3)** [for questions (2), offer chat (1)]
RFS (31)	- **real time contact (14)** [with person (10), with physician (4)] - **easy/fast access (5)** [to office (4), to physician (1)] - **extend hours (4)** - **more phone lines (4)** [direct to physician (2), add toll-free (2)] - **anytime access: on-call (3)** - **Online contact (1)**
AMED (1)	- **easy/fast access (1)**

Table 13. FAA accessibility issues/solutions (count) from the MFI group

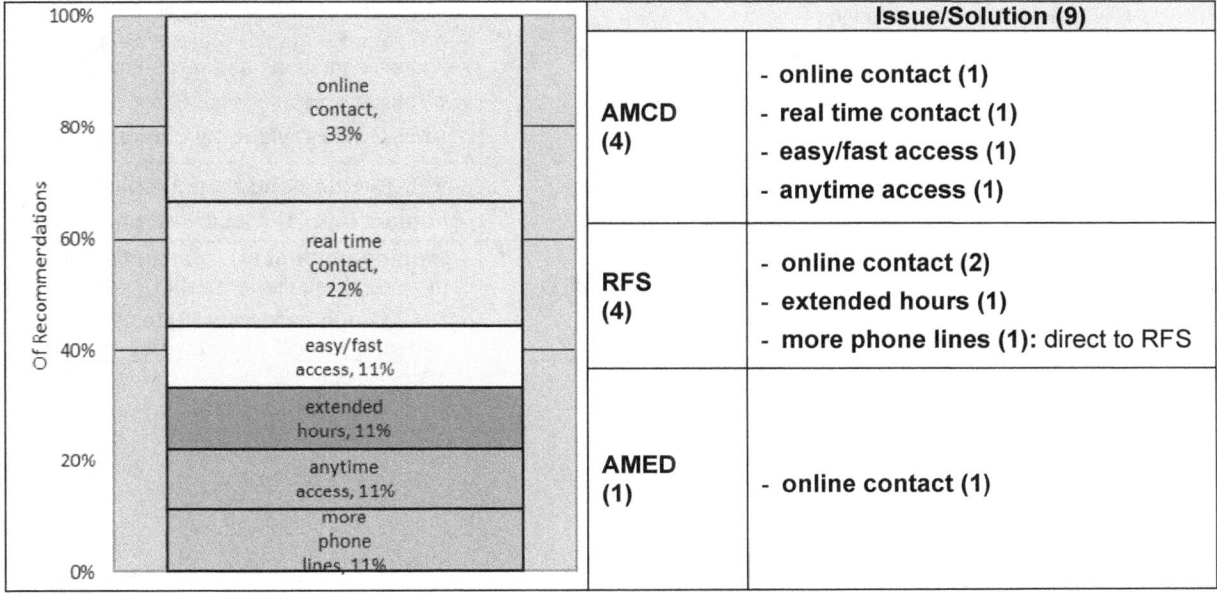

	Issue/Solution (9)
AMCD (4)	- **online contact (1)** - **real time contact (1)** - **easy/fast access (1)** - **anytime access (1)**
RFS (4)	- **online contact (2)** - **extended hours (1)** - **more phone lines (1)**: direct to RFS
AMED (1)	- **online contact (1)**

The groups raised similar issues—to be effective and efficient, they rely on guidance and decision making from FAA physicians and technical support for AMCS, in particular. At hand is that the need for assistance from AMCD is often during an exam or outside of FAA office hours, especially for AMEs in the Pacific Time Zone and abroad. For the domestic AMEs in six of the nine regions, difficulty making contact with RFS office staff was most frequently noted.

Information Request. AMEs expressed a need for information to help them do their jobs. The specifics are in Tables 14 and 15. The domestic AMEs had more variable information needs than the MFI group. The domestic group expressed a need for more reference materials as decision aids and material to assist airmen in meeting special issuance (SI) requirements, whereas, some from both groups expressed interest in information on ECG equipment.

The manner of distributing the requested information was not always specified; however, when it was noted, there was a tendency toward online access (11 of 17). If the information they need is currently available, then the request reveals that critical information is not reaching some AMEs, and further investigation may be warranted.

Communication (timeliness/content). A recurrent needed improvement at AMCD and the RFS offices (9 of the 11 are in the Southern region) was to be more responsive to AMEs; and for AMCD is to be more communicative. The MFI group's four recommendations pertained solely to AMCD—with three requests to be responsive to AMEs and one request to inform

Table 14. Information requests (count) from domestic AMEs

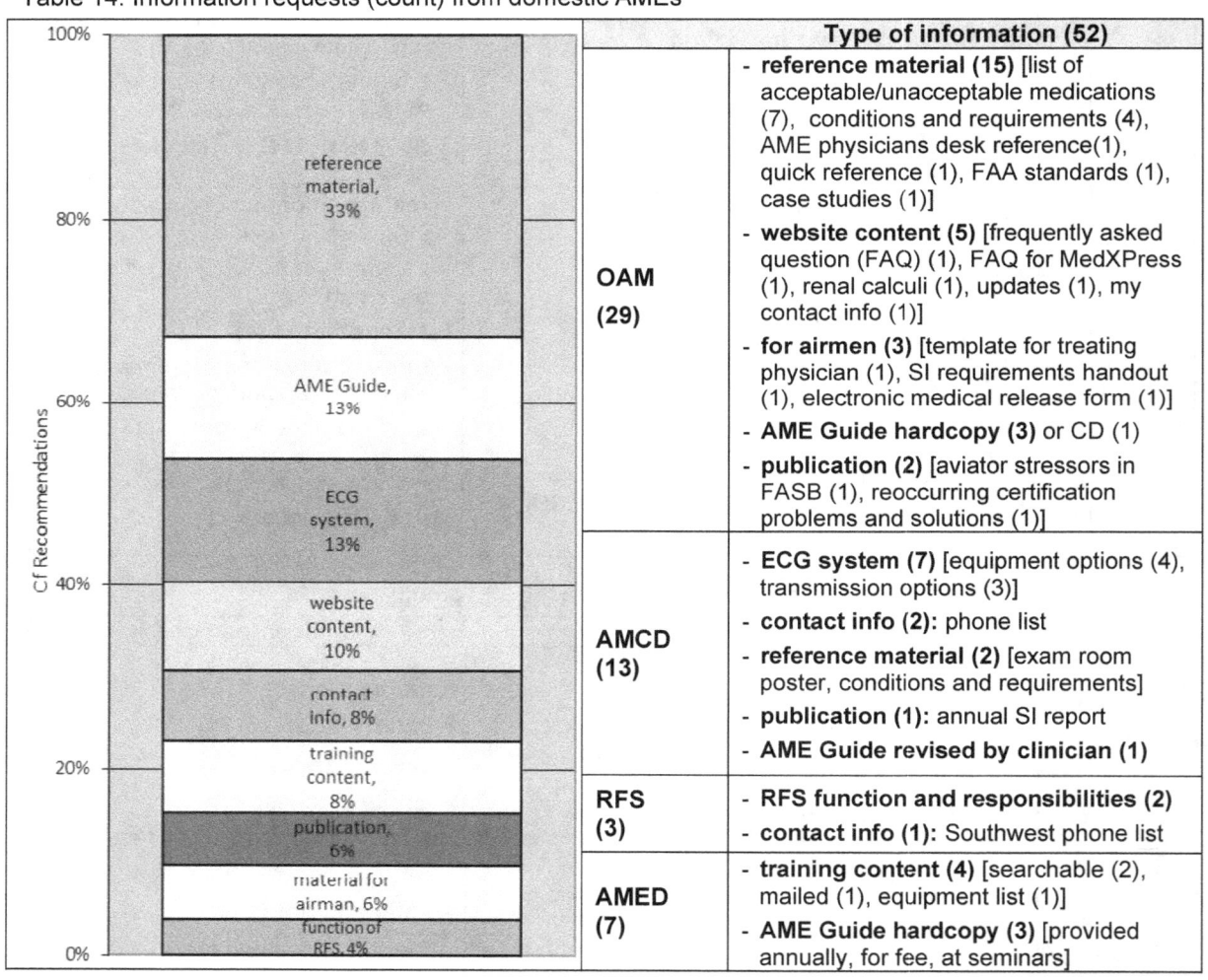

	Type of information (52)
OAM (29)	- **reference material (15)** [list of acceptable/unacceptable medications (7), conditions and requirements (4), AME physicians desk reference(1), quick reference (1), FAA standards (1), case studies (1)] - **website content (5)** [frequently asked question (FAQ) (1), FAQ for MedXPress (1), renal calculi (1), updates (1), my contact info (1)] - **for airmen (3)** [template for treating physician (1), SI requirements handout (1), electronic medical release form (1)] - **AME Guide hardcopy (3)** or CD (1) - **publication (2)** [aviator stressors in FASB (1), reoccurring certification problems and solutions (1)]
AMCD (13)	- **ECG system (7)** [equipment options (4), transmission options (3)] - **contact info (2)**: phone list - **reference material (2)** [exam room poster, conditions and requirements] - **publication (1)**: annual SI report - **AME Guide revised by clinician (1)**
RFS (3)	- **RFS function and responsibilities (2)** - **contact info (1)**: Southwest phone list
AMED (7)	- **training content (4)** [searchable (2), mailed (1), equipment list (1)] - **AME Guide hardcopy (3)** [provided annually, for fee, at seminars]

airmen regarding deferral timeframe. The domestic group's communication recommendations are shown in Table 16. Beyond their specified need for notification when certification policies change, confirmation of receipt of ECG transmissions, and information on training due dates; to improve their performance, several domestic AMEs asked for corrective feedback on their certification decisions and deferrals sent to AMCD. Some also asked that FAA communications with them and the airmen contain full details of requirements and decision timelines.

Table 15. Information requests (count) from the MFI group

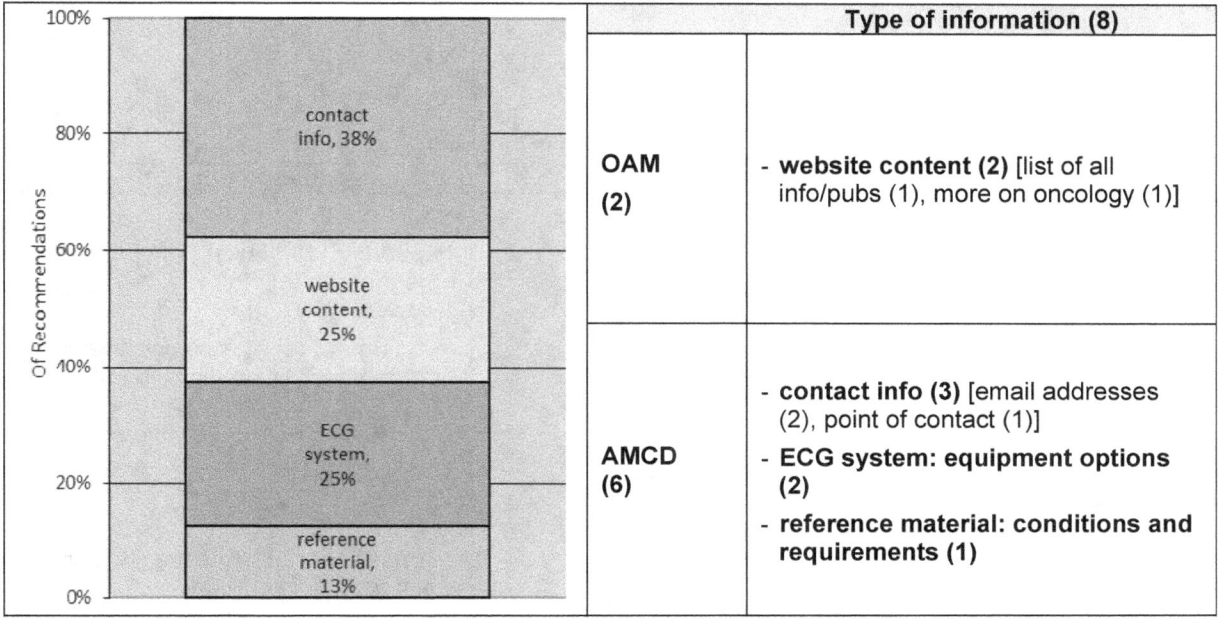

	Type of information (8)	
OAM (2)	- **website content (2)** [list of all info/pubs (1), more on oncology (1)]	
AMCD (6)	- **contact info (3)** [email addresses (2), point of contact (1)] - **ECG system: equipment options (2)** - **reference material: conditions and requirements (1)**	

Table 16. Communication issues/solutions (count) from domestic AMEs

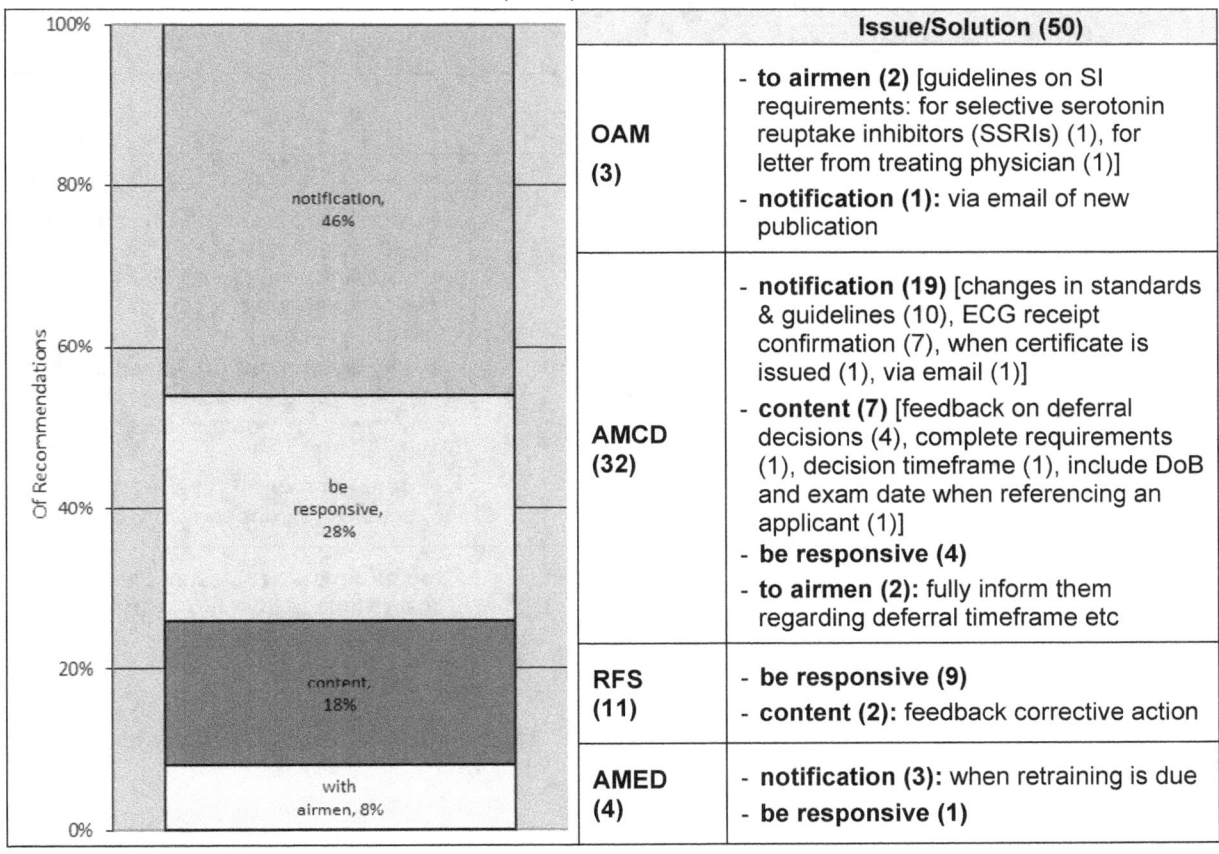

	Issue/Solution (50)
OAM (3)	- **to airmen (2)** [guidelines on SI requirements: for selective serotonin reuptake inhibitors (SSRIs) (1), for letter from treating physician (1)] - **notification (1):** via email of new publication
AMCD (32)	- **notification (19)** [changes in standards & guidelines (10), ECG receipt confirmation (7), when certificate is issued (1), via email (1)] - **content (7)** [feedback on deferral decisions (4), complete requirements (1), decision timeframe (1), include DoB and exam date when referencing an applicant (1)] - **be responsive (4)** - **to airmen (2):** fully inform them regarding deferral timeframe etc
RFS (11)	- **be responsive (9)** - **content (2):** feedback corrective action
AMED (4)	- **notification (3):** when retraining is due - **be responsive (1)**

FAA Decision. The three issues raised by the AME groups pertained to AMCD and their RFS office: (a) lack of consistency in decisions (across regions and FAA physicians), (b) too lengthy of a decision process for deferrals, and (c) need for decisiveness when calling for a decision or guidance. The MFI group's three recommendations were: two requests for faster turnaround from AMCD and an expressed need for decisiveness from the RFS office. The majority (18 of 20) of issues/solutions raised by the domestic group focused on AMCD. Specifics are presented in Table 17.

Cost. The two main issues raised by the AME groups were costs associated with time and travel for training and ECG equipment and transmission costs. The MFI group noted three issues/solutions: the costliness of ECG equipment and the need to reduce and/or cover training travel costs. Specific issues/solutions from the domestic group, presented in Table 18, are nearly evenly split between the ECG system and training.

Table 17. FAA decision issues/solutions (count) from domestic AMEs

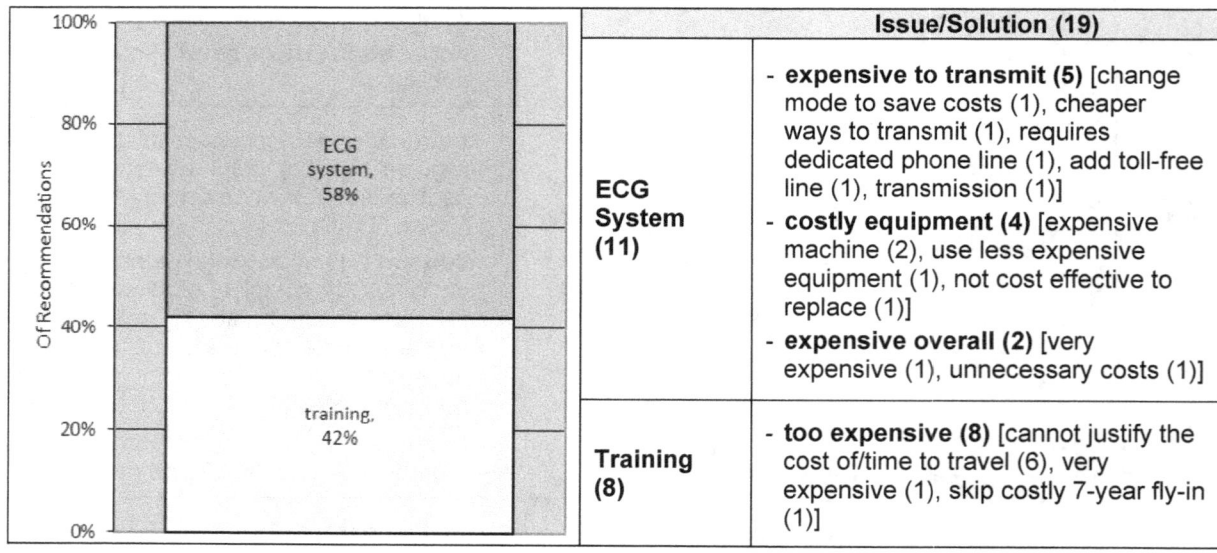

		Issue/Solution (20)
	AMCD 18)	- **speedier (13)** [faster (7), streamline the process (4), no more than 4 weeks (3)] - **consistent (5)** [across physicians (2), regions (1), predictable (1)]
	RFS 2)	- **consistent (1):** across regions and with AMCD - **decisive (1)**

Table 18. Cost issues/solutions (count) from domestic AMEs

		Issue/Solution (19)
	ECG System (11)	- **expensive to transmit (5)** [change mode to save costs (1), cheaper ways to transmit (1), requires dedicated phone line (1), add toll-free line (1), transmission (1)] - **costly equipment (4)** [expensive machine (2), use less expensive equipment (1), not cost effective to replace (1)] - **expensive overall (2)** [very expensive (1), unnecessary costs (1)]
	Training (8)	- **too expensive (8)** [cannot justify the cost of/time to travel (6), very expensive (1), skip costly 7-year fly-in (1)]

FAA Personnel. Issues/solutions raised by domestic AMEs concerned the need for more FAA personnel and service-oriented support. Specifics are presented in Table 19. The MFI group did not raise any issues with FAA personnel.

Summary of Results for Development of Organizational Capability. Tables 20 and 21 contain summaries of the 330 AME recommendations for developing organizational capability. Table 20 provides a programmatic perspective by showing the breakout of feedback within each category across the organizations serving AMEs. Table 21 provides the individual organizations a perspective on which capabilities need improving by showing the distribution of recommendations across feedback categories.

Highlights in Table 20 indicate the organizational level where the majority of recommended improvements reside for each feedback category. Most of the feedback pertained to AMCD (Table 21), which is not surprising, given they are more likely to have contact with AMEs, as noted earlier in the report. AMEs proposed on-call physicians and online contact as possible solutions to the lack of timely guidance and decision making from AMCD. They also expressed issues with the responsiveness of AMCD in providing notification of changes in standards and guidelines, deferral status, and receipt of supporting documentation, in particular, and seemingly slow, inconsistent decision making process for deferrals, in general. Expenses associated with conducting ECGs were noted more than the cost to attend training, with changes in transmission mode and equipment proposed as cost reducing solutions. The need for development of FAA personnel was indicated particularly in the amount and quality of interactions with RFS staff. Information requests were mainly for decision aids and form templates, a change that warrants review by OAM.

Table 19. FAA personnel issues/solutions (count) from domestic AMEs

Table 20. Breakout of each feedback category across service providers

	(Shading indicates highest percent in each feedback category.)						
	Training need	FAA accessibility	Information request	FAA communication	FAA decision	Cost	FAA personnel
OAM	12%	--	52%	5%	--	--	--
AMCD	--	51%	32%	67%	87%	64% ECG System	33%
RFS	--	46%	5%	20%	13%	--	59%
AMED	76% AME 13% airman	3%	11%	8%	--	36% AME training	8%
Total count*	68	76	60	54	23	22	27

*Total count is the sum of the number of recommendations from both groups; therefore, a greater contribution from the MFI group to the cumulative percent will result in a smaller count than the reverse.

17

Regarding AME training offered by AMED, beyond the specific content/subject matter AMEs requested, they also indicated the need for variable training locations, more offerings, and on-demand training. Online training such as self-paced, multimedia courses and webinars would help reduce training costs AMEs incur, and, when done right, could support some of their recommended instructional methods (e.g., case studies, demonstration, small group discussion, and speakers).

3.3.2 Enhancements to Systems/Tools

The analysis examined a subset of 191 recommendations relevant to the digital ECG System, AMCS, MedXPress, online AME Guide, and OAM website—systems/tools AMEs rely on to perform their duties as FAA designees. There were distinct differences between the groups (Table 22), which likely reflects differences in levels of experience with the various systems/tools. The domestic AMEs recommended improvements across the board, while the MFI group focused on three systems/tools.

The actionable feedback categories, defined in Table 23, are pertinent to designing digital systems/tools for effective and efficient use and are referred to as "ilities." The categories are the common themes for needed improvements to systems/tools that emerged during the content analysis. It is important to note that the *ilities* are not mutually interdependent. For instance, an interface may be easy to navigate and intuitive, but unless the system/tool effectively supports the user in meeting job requirements, it will have limited utility. The same goes for a system/tool that cannot be consistently accessed or is unstable once accessed—it has limited utility—unreliable systems/tools also introduce unnecessary frustrations.

Table 21. Distribution of recommendations for each service provider

(Total count*)	Training need	FAA accessibility	Information request	FAA communication	FAA decision	Cost	FAA personnel
AMCD (137)	--	28%	14%	26%	15%	10%	7%
AMED (83)	72%	2%	8%	5%	--	10%	2%
RFS (68)		51%	4%	4%	4%		24%
OAM (42)	19%	--	74%	7%	--	--	--

*Total count is the sum of the number of recommendations from both groups.

Table 22. Distribution (percent) of recommendations across systems/tools

	AMCS	ECG System	MedXPress	Online AME Guide	OAM Website
Domestic AMEs (170 recommendations)	34.1	20.0	29.4	8.8	7.6
MFI group (21 recommendations)	76.2	19.0	---	4.8	---

Table 23. Actionable feedback categories for enhancing systems/tools

Add capability	- add function/feature not currently supported
Adjust capability	- change to function currently supported - change to existing interface feature (e.g., button, text box, menu)
Reliability	- server/software needs to be available and stable - transmission failures need to be reduced and availability improved - input accurately displayed/saved
Usability	- make the interface/printouts easier to use to accomplish tasks - make more user friendly
Utility	- support users in effectively/successfully performing required tasks - support practical electronic transmission modes - address challenges to end users (e.g., computer access and skills)

The distribution of recommendations across the categories is presented in Figure 7.

The next phase of the analysis involved assigning secondary categories and computing their frequencies. Detailed results follow for the feedback categories, going from highest to lowest cumulative percent (Fig 7). As a reminder, some recommended improvements are stated as issues or problem areas that need addressing and others are stated as solutions. Results in this section's tables are ordered highest to lowest frequency from top to bottom row.

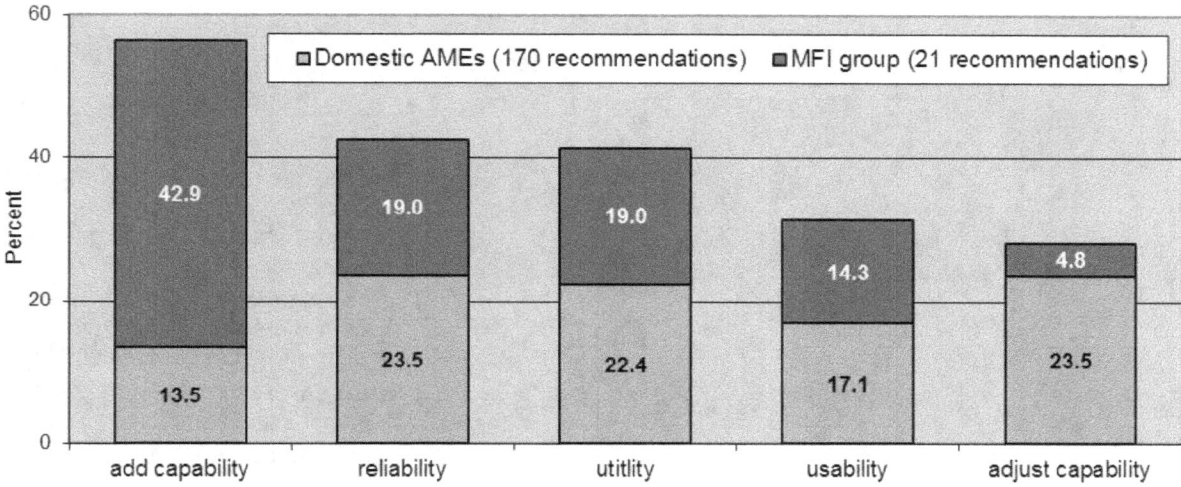

Figure 7. Distribution of feedback on enhancing systems/tools

Add Capability. The AME groups identified embedded guidance in AMCS for themselves and in MedXPress for the airmen (Tables 24 and 25) as the main improvement to the systems/tools. The embedded guidance would expedite the application process by (a) reducing airmen application errors, which take time for AMEs to correct and explain; (b) reducing calls to the RFS office and AMCD, with appropriate guidance to aid AME decisions; and (c) educating airmen on needed supporting documentation for their medical conditions and AMEs on updates to certification standards and guidelines.

Table 24. "Add capability" issues/solutions (count) from domestic AMEs

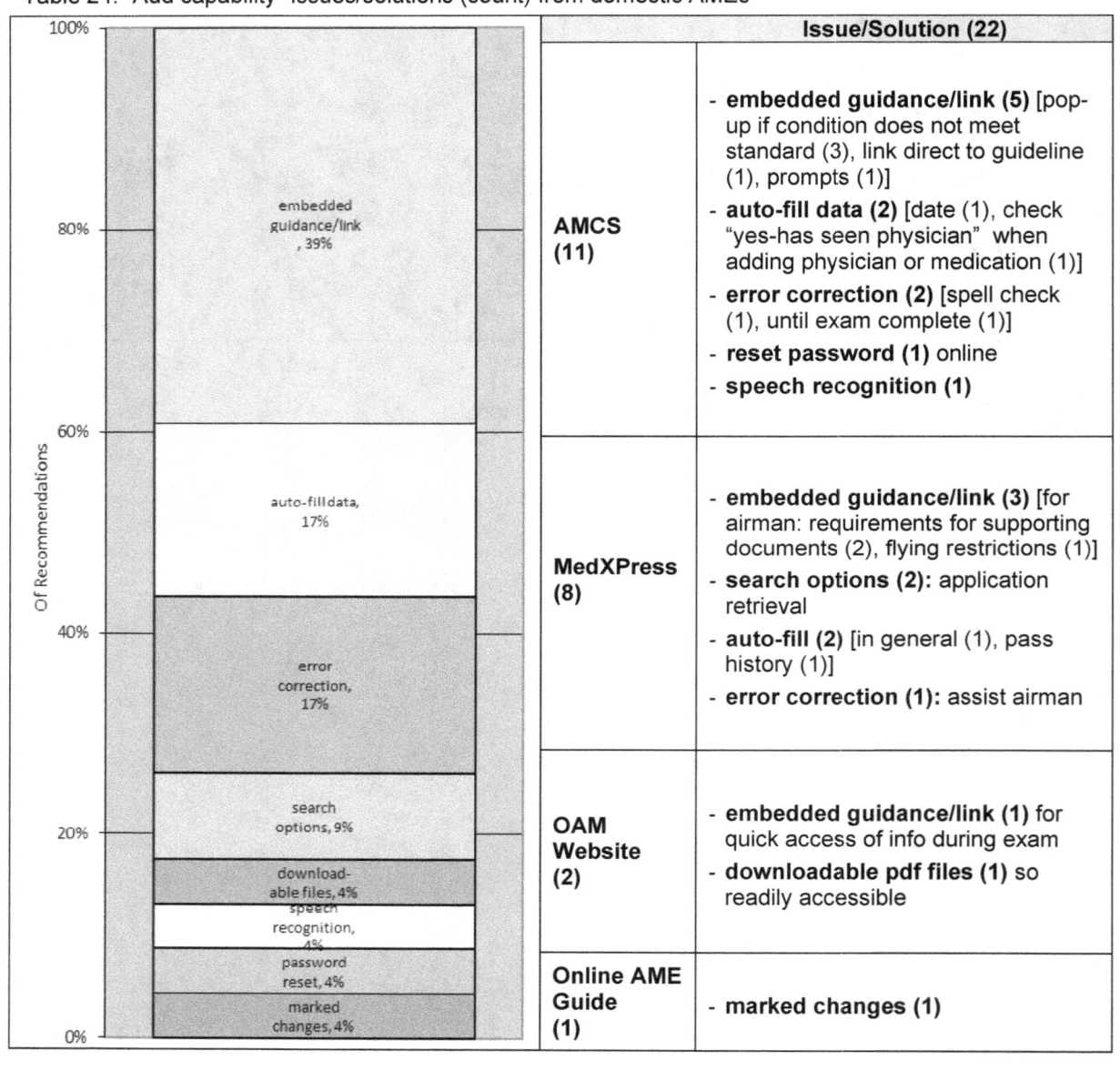

	Issue/Solution (22)
AMCS (11)	- **embedded guidance/link (5)** [pop-up if condition does not meet standard (3), link direct to guideline (1), prompts (1)] - **auto-fill data (2)** [date (1), check "yes-has seen physician" when adding physician or medication (1)] - **error correction (2)** [spell check (1), until exam complete (1)] - **reset password (1)** online - **speech recognition (1)**
MedXPress (8)	- **embedded guidance/link (3)** [for airman: requirements for supporting documents (2), flying restrictions (1)] - **search options (2)**: application retrieval - **auto-fill (2)** [in general (1), pass history (1)] - **error correction (1)**: assist airman
OAM Website (2)	- **embedded guidance/link (1)** for quick access of info during exam - **downloadable pdf files (1)** so readily accessible
Online AME Guide (1)	- **marked changes (1)**

Table 25. "Add capability" issues/solutions (count) from the MFI group

	Issue/Solution (9)
	AMCS (8) - **embedded guidance (4)** [warning/link given airman history (2), suggestions while completing form (1), better link to AME guide (1)] - **view certificate (2)** [before final (1), button (1)] - **add button (2)** [SUBMIT (1), tech support contact info (1)]
	Online AME Guide (1) - **Track changes (1):** to print out

Reliability. AMEs brought attention to their need for systems/tools that are trustworthy, i.e., accessible on-demand and stable once accessed, with no concern for data integrity (once entered, not subject to corruption or loss). All four reliability issues raised by the MFI group pertained to improving the stability and data integrity of AMCS. The domestic group addressed reliability issues with AMCS, MedXPress, and ECG transmission (Table 26). They are asking for alternative means of completing data entry off-line when systems are unavailable to eliminate slowdowns and frustrations.

Table 26. Reliability issues/solutions (count) from domestic AMEs

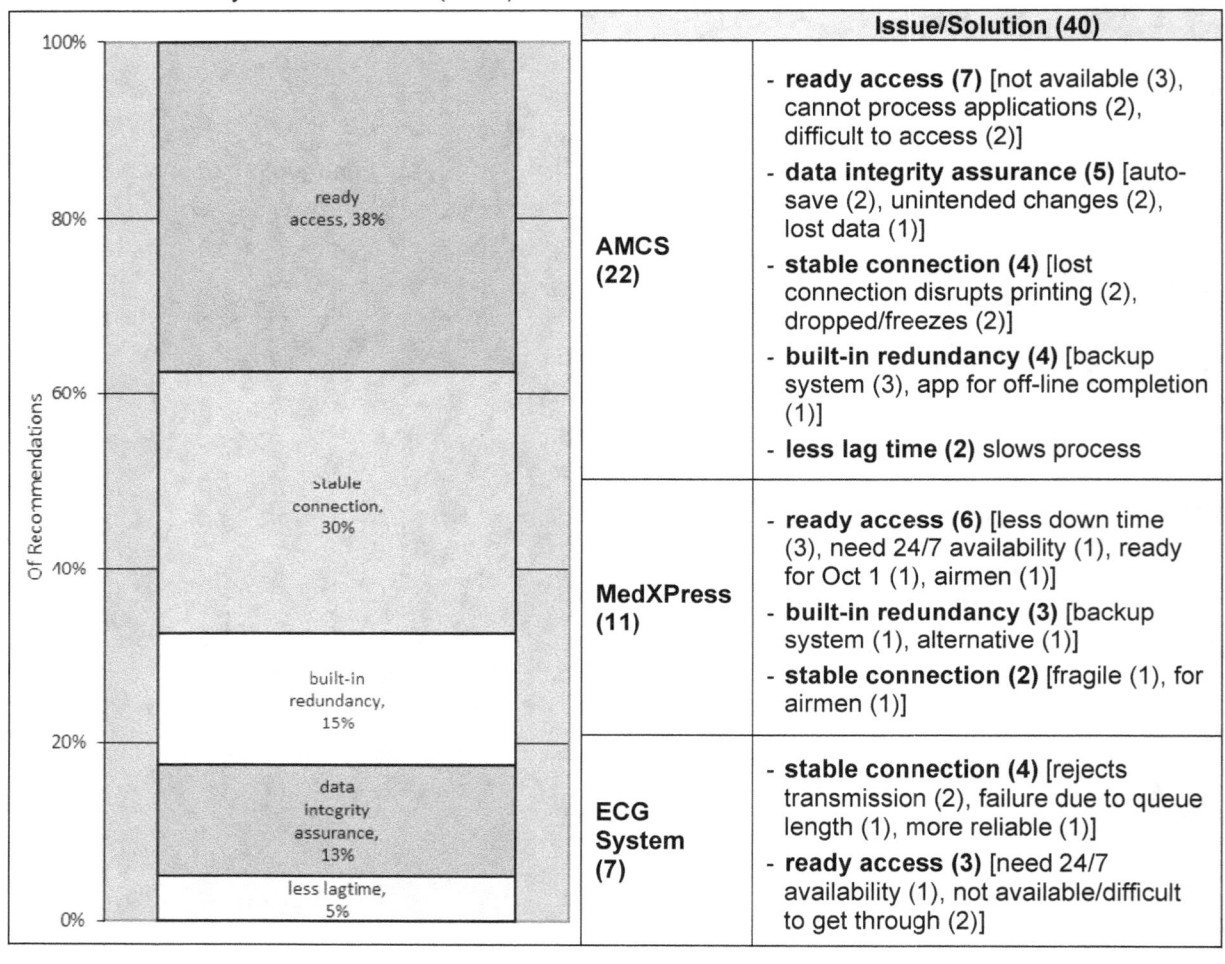

	Issue/Solution (40)
AMCS (22)	- **ready access (7)** [not available (3), cannot process applications (2), difficult to access (2)] - **data integrity assurance (5)** [auto-save (2), unintended changes (2), lost data (1)] - **stable connection (4)** [lost connection disrupts printing (2), dropped/freezes (2)] - **built-in redundancy (4)** [backup system (3), app for off-line completion (1)] - **less lag time (2)** slows process
MedXPress (11)	- **ready access (6)** [less down time (3), need 24/7 availability (1), ready for Oct 1 (1), airmen (1)] - **built-in redundancy (3)** [backup system (1), alternative (1)] - **stable connection (2)** [fragile (1), for airmen (1)]
ECG System (7)	- **stable connection (4)** [rejects transmission (2), failure due to queue length (1), more reliable (1)] - **ready access (3)** [need 24/7 availability (1), not available/difficult to get through (2)]

Utility. The AME groups mainly focused on enhancing the utility of the ECG System by modernizing equipment, in particular, to accept various types of digital files. The four recommendations from the MFI group pertained to digital transmission modes for ECGs, with one specifying transmission via the Internet. Recommendations of multiple acceptable transmission modes from the domestic group, detailed in Table 27, included: use of Internet Protocol (IP) to transmit over a high-speed network instead of a telephone line (see http://transition.fcc.gov/voip/), upload to an Internet site using a File Transfer Protocol (FTP) or Hyper Text Transfer Protocol (HTTP) files, upload directly to AMCS, fax, or scan and send as an email attachment. Depending on how it is implemented, special equipment/software may be required to securely send and receive transmissions over the Internet or via fax.

Table 27. Utility issues/solutions (count) from domestic AMEs

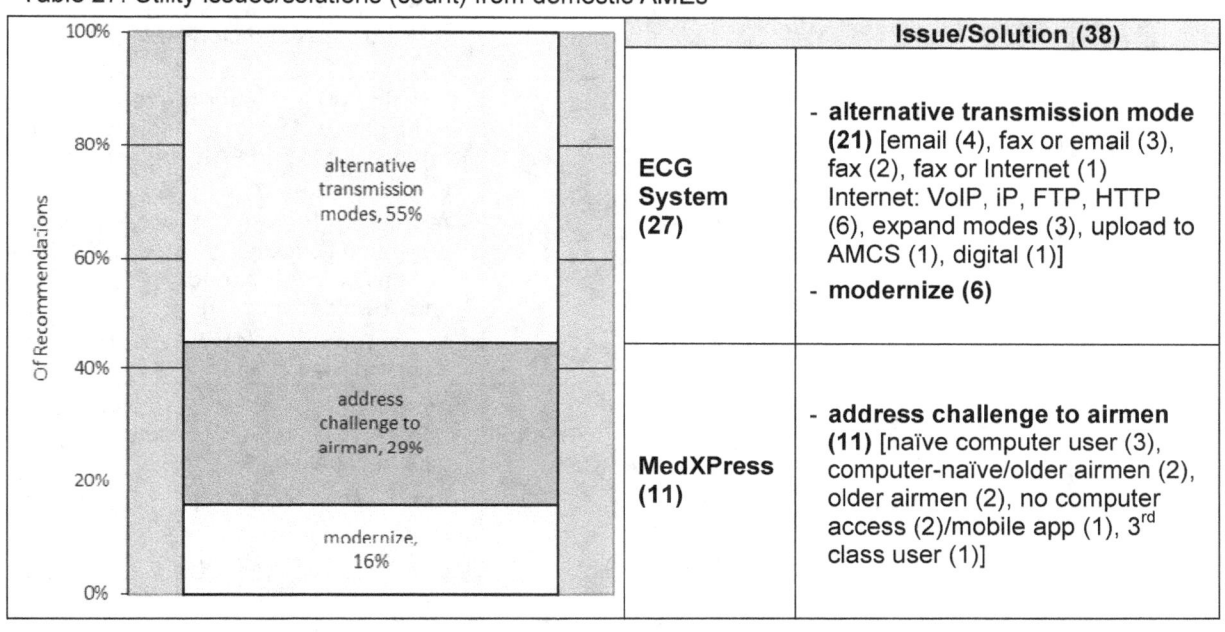

In addition, the domestic AMEs noted challenges MedX-Press presents to the airmen who have limited or no computer access and minimal or no computer experience, which may be partly due to generational differences in the airman population.

Usability. Improving usability of the digital systems/tools, for the most part, reduces the burden on the user. The domestic AME recommendations, presented in Table 28, involved minimizing interactions with the systems/tools through ease of access to information and navigation, streamlining procedures, and reducing information overload. The MFI group's three usability issues focused on AMCS—too time consuming, needs to be easier to correct errors, and needs to be easier to explain corrections made to the airman's application.

Table 28. Usability issues/solutions (count) from domestic AMEs

	Issue/Solution (29)
Online AME Guide (8)	- **more user friendly (5)** [easier to use (2), easier to navigate (2), easier access medical info (1)] - **simplify (3)** [quick link/easier access (2), add index and cross referencing (1)]
OAM Website (8)	- **simplify (4)** [unclutter (1), reduce redundancy (1), info in single location (1), difficult to find FAA contact info (1)] - **more user friendly (3)** [easier to navigate (1), easier to use online help (1), easier for airman to find/download info (1)] - **larger font/print (1)** make bulletin easier to read online
AMCS (7)	- **simplify (3)** [in general (1), steps to print (1), reduce burden of quarterly user verification (1)] - **more user friendly (2)** - **larger font/print (2)** [larger (1), MID and ID# on printout (1)]
MedXPress (6)	- **larger font/print (3)** - **simplify (2)**: printing steps - **more user friendly (1)** confusing for initial airman user

The chart on the left (Of Recommendations, 0%–100%) shows: simplify, 41%; more user friendly, 38%; larger font, 21%.

Adjust Capability. Some of the existing capabilities require adjustments to reduce user frustrations, better support AMEs, and address challenges reported by airmen. The MFI group had a single recommendation, which was to extend AMCS's lockout time. The domestic group indicated similar issues and changes to better meet certification requirements for completing and submitting applications and a single improvement for the online tools (Table 29). Their recommendation to improve the search capability for the online tools would provide them access to the right information on-demand. Needed improvements to AMCS and MedXPress would better support requirements by (a) extending time before locking out the user, (b) easing password requirements, and (c) adjusting interface features to minimize constraints on AME input and place constraints on airman input. Since lockout times are regulated for government systems, use of a warning (pop-up or auditory), as suggested,

Table 29. "Adjust capability" issues/solutions (count) from domestic AMEs

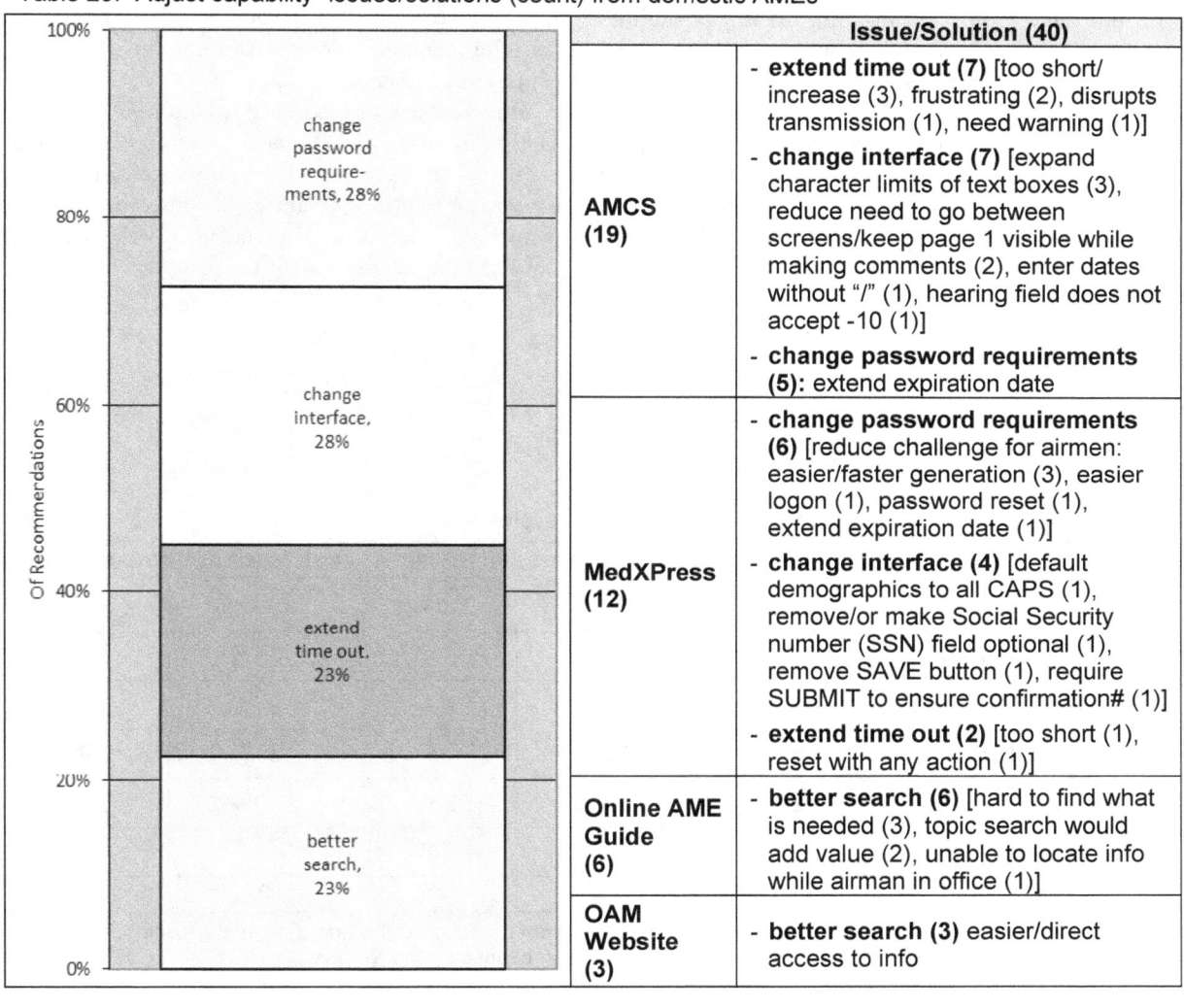

	Issue/Solution (40)
AMCS (19)	- **extend time out (7)** [too short/increase (3), frustrating (2), disrupts transmission (1), need warning (1)] - **change interface (7)** [expand character limits of text boxes (3), reduce need to go between screens/keep page 1 visible while making comments (2), enter dates without "/" (1), hearing field does not accept -10 (1)] - **change password requirements (5):** extend expiration date
MedXPress (12)	- **change password requirements (6)** [reduce challenge for airmen: easier/faster generation (3), easier logon (1), password reset (1), extend expiration date (1)] - **change interface (4)** [default demographics to all CAPS (1), remove/or make Social Security number (SSN) field optional (1), remove SAVE button (1), require SUBMIT to ensure confirmation# (1)] - **extend time out (2)** [too short (1), reset with any action (1)]
Online AME Guide (6)	- **better search (6)** [hard to find what is needed (3), topic search would add value (2), unable to locate info while airman in office (1)]
OAM Website (3)	- **better search (3)** easier/direct access to info

may be the practical solution.

Summary of Results for Enhancements to Systems/Tools. Tables 30 and 31 contain summaries of the 191 AME recommendations for enhancing digital systems/tools. Table 30 provides a programmatic perspective by showing the breakout of feedback within each category across the systems/tools.

Highlights in Table 30 indicate the system/tool receiving the majority of recommended improvements within a feedback category, with AMCS receiving the most overall. Thus, enhancements to AMCS would likely provide the most benefit, especially in terms of adding new capabilities, such as embedding guidance or decision aids and creating, and adjusting existing capabilities to better support AME tasks, as well as improving the readiness of the system for high rates of use, ensuring the integrity of entered data, and making it more user friendly.

Similar needed improvements to MedXPress would benefit AME and airman users, to include addressing the challenge it poses to airmen with limited computer access and experience. Noteworthy is the absence of recommendations for improving the usefulness of the OAM website, online AME guide, and AMCS. To the contrary, there is a high rate of recommendations to improve the usefulness of the ECG system.

Table 31 provides the individual organizations a perspective on needed improvements to their particular system/tool by showing the distribution of recommendations.

3.3.3 Changes to Processes and Policies

The analysis examined a subset of 170 recommendations involving change to the medical certification processes (e.g., application, examination, submission, and issuance decision) and change to the medical certification program policies (e.g., rules governing AMEs and their authority, airman application requirements, requirements of medical certification classes, and controlled Form 8500-8 and paper certificates). Often there is not a clear line between process and policy; thus, that determination will be left to responsible parties in OAM.

The problems raised and/or solutions presented involve changes in the *who, what, when, where, and how* airman medical certificates are issued. In certain instances, a recommendation may appear to belong to one of the other high-level categories, because its implementation would ultimately involve the agency providing the service, system/tool support, or both.

Table 30. Breakout of each feedback category across systems/tools

	(Shading indicates highest percent in each feedback category.)				
	Add capability	Reliability	Utility	Usability	Adjust capability
OAM Website	6.5%	--	--	25%	7%
Online AME Guide	6.5%	--	--	25%	15%
AMCS	61%	60%	--	31%	49%
MedXPress	26%	25%	26%	19%	29%
ECG System	--	16%	74%	--	--
Total count*	31	44	42	32	41

*Total count is the sum of the number of recommendations from both groups; therefore, a greater contribution from the MFI group to the cumulative percent will result in a smaller count than the reverse.

Table 31. Distribution of recommendations for each system/tool

(Total count*)	Add capability	Reliability	Utility	Usability	Adjust capability
AMCS (74)	27%	34%	--	14%	26%
MedXPress (50)	16%	24%	22%	12%	26%
ECG System (38)	--	18%	82%	--	--
Online AME Guide (16)	13%	--	--	50%	38%
OAM Website (13)	15%	--	--	62%	23%

*Total count is the sum of the number of recommendations from both groups.

The five of the six actionable feedback categories, defined in Table 32, align with stages in the medical certification process. The sixth feedback category covers FAA rules governing AMEs. Figure 8 shows the distribution of recommendations across the categories.

In the next phase of the analysis, frequencies were computed for the secondary category assignments. Detailed results are presented differently here on two fronts. First, the table rows align with the graphic, since the secondary categories mapped directly onto the needed change. Second, AME feedback on deferral tracking and standards and guidelines is respectively included under results for *Transmission to the* FAA and *Certification Decision*. Feedback on certification requirements for mainly third-class medical certificates is also under *Certification Decision*.

Table 32. Actionable feedback categories for process/policy change

Airman application	- applicant access to previously entered medical history - change to items 1-20 on Form 8500-8 - MedXPress requirement
AME rule	- conduct of exam - minimum exams per year - location restriction
Exam appointment	- change to items 21-64 on Form 8500-8 - timing of AME access to application - AME review of FAA record on airman (e.g., previously submitted medical history, past exam report, correspondence)
Certification decision	- AME decision authority - temporary certificate
Printed certificate	- type of paper - reprint certificate
Transmission to the FAA	- type of acceptable format (e.g., digital, paper, fax) - deadline to submit supporting documentation - retrieval of submission for error correction

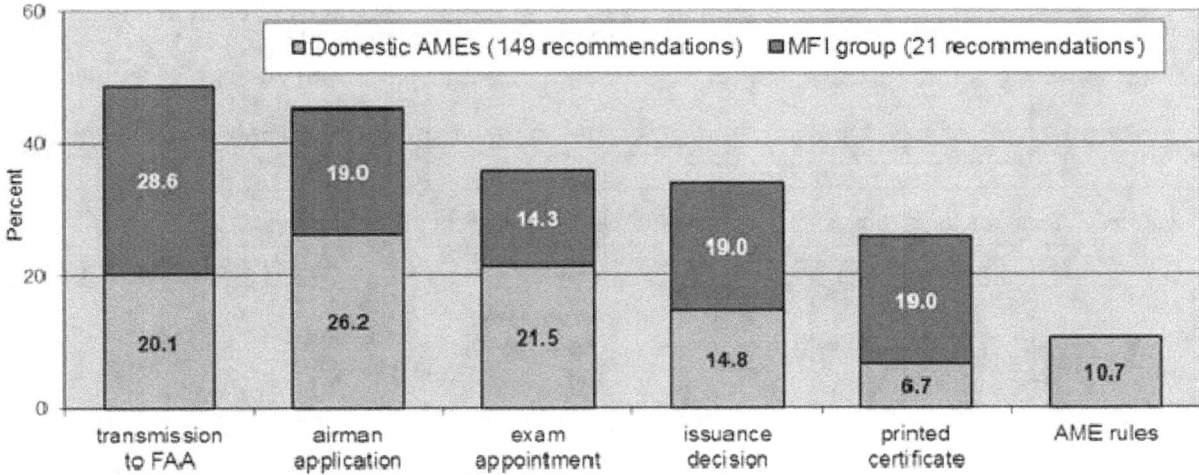

Figure 8. Distribution of feedback on process/policy change

Transmission to the FAA. Recommendations mainly focused on the need to electronically transmit completed exams and supporting documentation. Half of the recommendations from Domestic AMEs (Table 33) and two-thirds from the MFI group (Table 34) supported moving toward paperless transmission. The proposed solutions included means to: Send a scanned file of the completed packet or scanned supporting documentation; upload electronic files to an Internet site; and either attach electronic files to email or AMCS, or scan them directly into AMCS. A point made by the MFI group was the seemingly redundant requirement to mail/fax completed exams and documents that had been electronically transmitted. AMEs from both groups also expressed a need to retrieve submissions in AMCS to either correct or add to the report.

Table 33. Changes to transmission processes/policies (count) from domestic AMEs

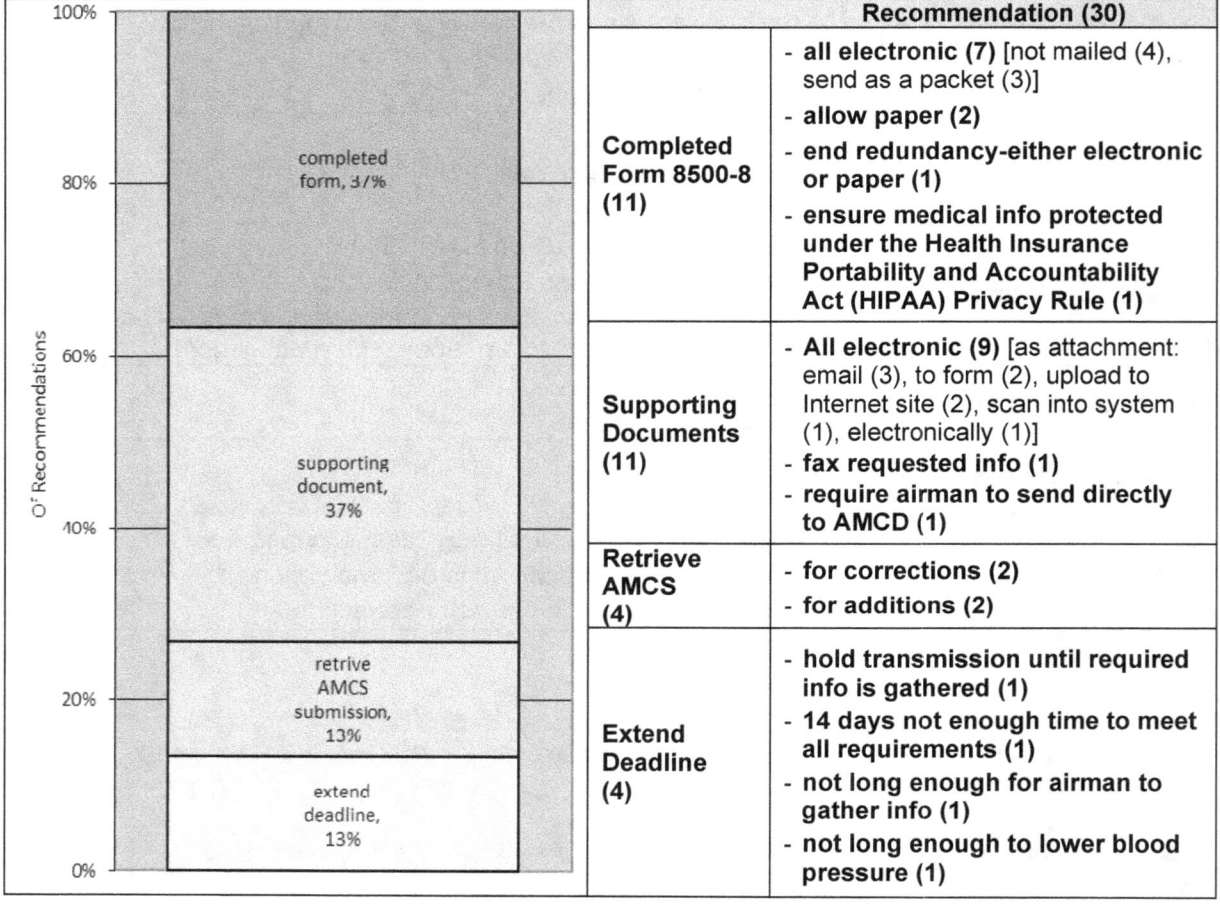

	Recommendation (30)
Completed Form 8500-8 (11)	- **all electronic (7)** [not mailed (4), send as a packet (3)] - **allow paper (2)** - **end redundancy-either electronic or paper (1)** - **ensure medical info protected under the Health Insurance Portability and Accountability Act (HIPAA) Privacy Rule (1)**
Supporting Documents (11)	- **All electronic (9)** [as attachment: email (3), to form (2), upload to Internet site (2), scan into system (1), electronically (1)] - **fax requested info (1)** - **require airman to send directly to AMCD (1)**
Retrieve AMCS (4)	- **for corrections (2)** - **for additions (2)**
Extend Deadline (4)	- **hold transmission until required info is gathered (1)** - **14 days not enough time to meet all requirements (1)** - **not long enough for airman to gather info (1)** - **not long enough to lower blood pressure (1)**

Table 34. Changes to transmission processes/policies (count) from the MFI group

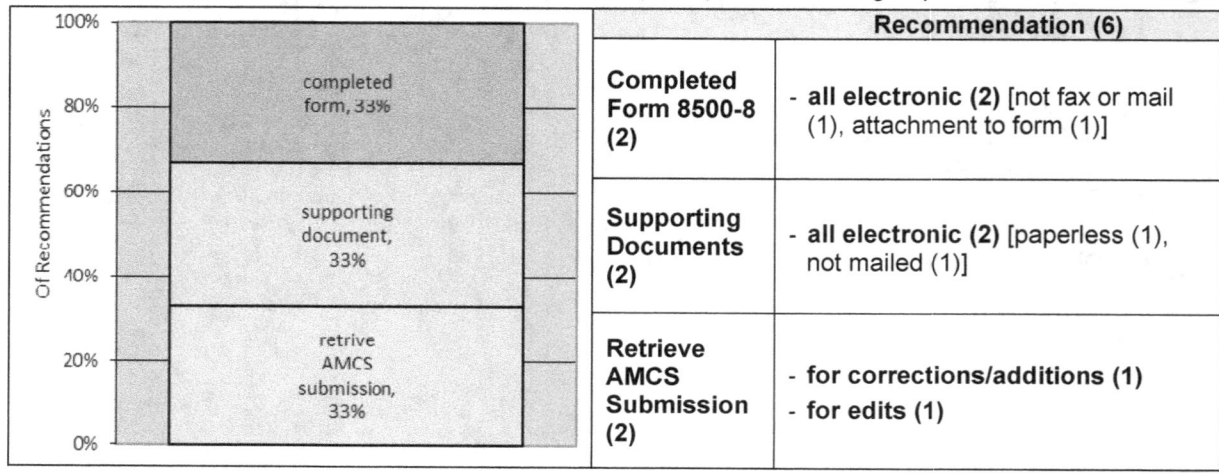

	Recommendation (6)
Completed Form 8500-8 (2)	- **all electronic (2)** [not fax or mail (1), attachment to form (1)]
Supporting Documents (2)	- **all electronic (2)** [paperless (1), not mailed (1)]
Retrieve AMCS Submission (2)	- **for corrections/additions (1)** - **for edits (1)**

Deferral Tracking. The domestic and MFI groups identified the need for a means of tracking the deferral process and the final decision. The two recommendations from the MFI group suggested the use of email. The four recommendations from the domestic group included an online capability (2), use of email (1), and emphasis on the criticality of providing the AME and airman a tracking service to monitor a deferral's progress (1).

Airman Application. Recommendations focused on the medical history page of Form 8500-8 (items 1-20) and related changes to airman use of MedXPress to apply for an airman medical certificate. The MFI group's three recommendations pertained to MedXPress: Offer it as an option (2) and remove the online form's response to a "Berlin" address, since Germany is united (1). The majority of the domestic group's changes (Table 35) focused on reducing applicant errors by adjusting wording and highlighting items 17, 18, and 19 and by allowing airmen to access and/or reuse input on past applications.

Table 35. Changes to application processes/policies (count) from domestic AMEs

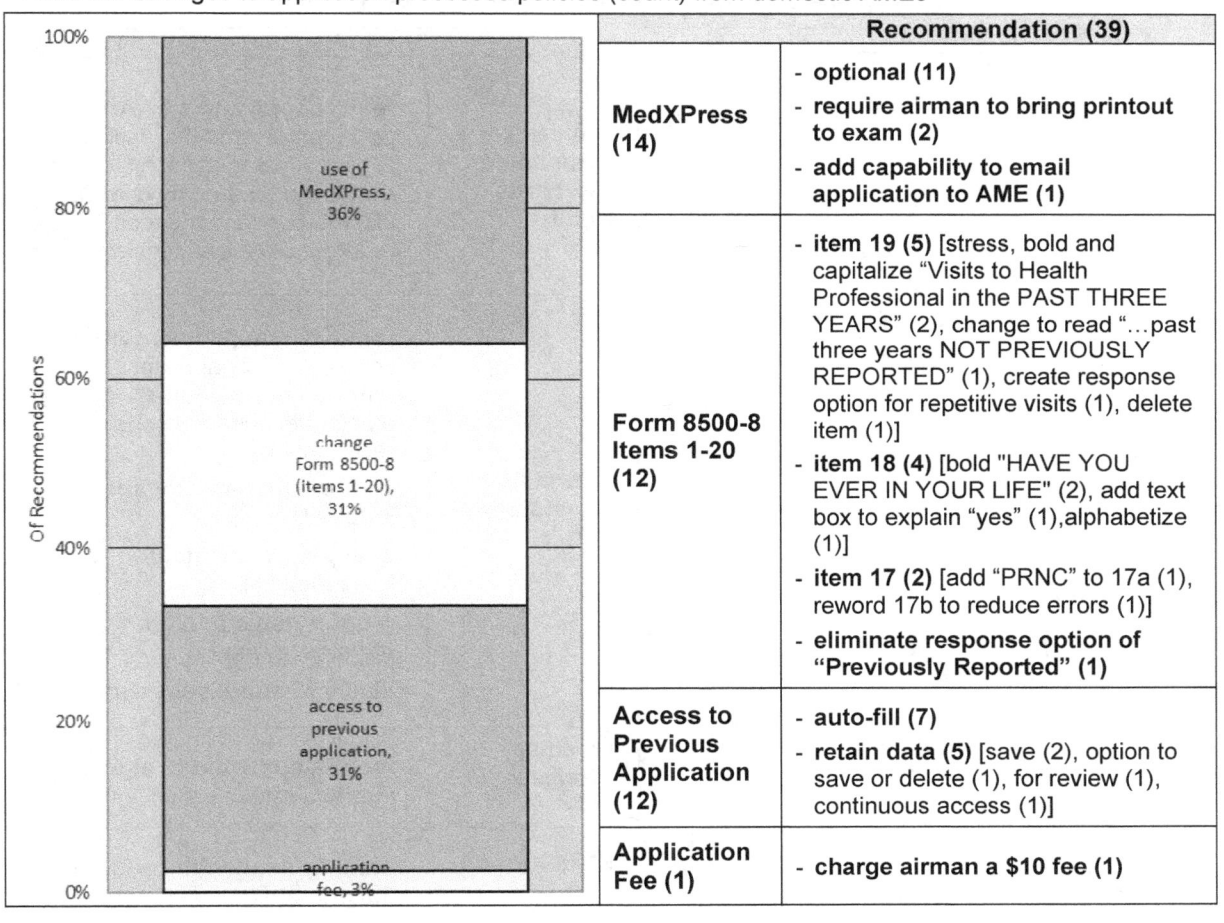

	Recommendation (39)
MedXPress (14)	- **optional (11)** - **require airman to bring printout to exam (2)** - **add capability to email application to AME (1)**
Form 8500-8 Items 1-20 (12)	- **item 19 (5)** [stress, bold and capitalize "Visits to Health Professional in the PAST THREE YEARS" (2), change to read "...past three years NOT PREVIOUSLY REPORTED" (1), create response option for repetitive visits (1), delete item (1)] - **item 18 (4)** [bold "HAVE YOU EVER IN YOUR LIFE" (2), add text box to explain "yes" (1),alphabetize (1)] - **item 17 (2)** [add "PRNC" to 17a (1), reword 17b to reduce errors (1)] - **eliminate response option of "Previously Reported" (1)**
Access to Previous Application (12)	- **auto-fill (7)** - **retain data (5)** [save (2), option to save or delete (1), for review (1), continuous access (1)]
Application Fee (1)	- **charge airman a $10 fee (1)**

Exam Appointment. Recommendations, for the most part, focused on changes that would reduce AME errors by providing them with full information on the applicant in their office and affect entering information into the examiner's portion of Form 8500-8 (items 21-64), which completes the form, via AMCS. Most often recommended by the MFI group (4 of 4) and domestic AMEs (Table 36) was access to applicant's medical certification records for review in preparation for the exam. A new requirement for applicants to sign a medical release form to allow their AME to view their records was also proposed.

Certification Decision. Recommendations mainly pertained to reducing deferrals by expanding the authority of the AME. Also proposed to better serve airman under certain circumstances was expanding AME authority through the issuance of temporary medical certificates.

Table 36. Changes to exam preparation and conduct (count) from domestic AMEs

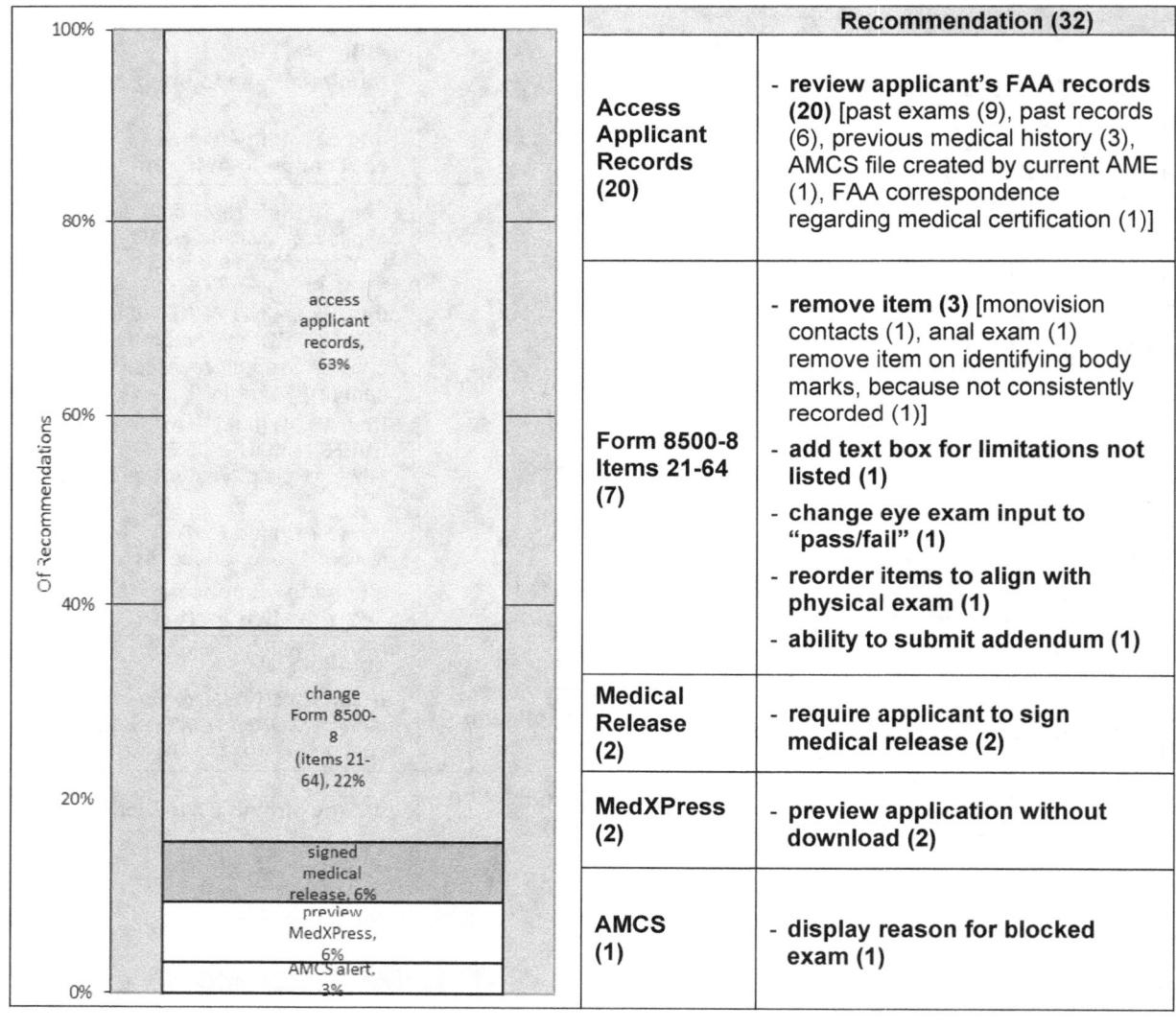

	Recommendation (32)
Access Applicant Records (20)	- **review applicant's FAA records (20)** [past exams (9), past records (6), previous medical history (3), AMCS file created by current AME (1), FAA correspondence regarding medical certification (1)]
Form 8500-8 Items 21-64 (7)	- **remove item (3)** [monovision contacts (1), anal exam (1) remove item on identifying body marks, because not consistently recorded (1)] - **add text box for limitations not listed (1)** - **change eye exam input to "pass/fail" (1)** - **reorder items to align with physical exam (1)** - **ability to submit addendum (1)**
Medical Release (2)	- **require applicant to sign medical release (2)**
MedXPress (2)	- **preview application without download (2)**
AMCS (1)	- **display reason for blocked exam (1)**

Chart labels: access applicant records, 63%; change Form 8500-8 (items 21-64), 22%; signed medical release, 6%; preview MedXPress, 6%; AMCS alert, 3%. Y-axis: Of Recommendations.

Three of the four recommendations from the MFI group would expand authority of: the RFS, the AME for SI cases requiring monitoring, and the senior AME with advanced AME-Assisted SI (AASI) training. Their fourth recommendation was to issue shorter, temporary medical certification for disease monitoring. The domestic group recommended qualified AMEs be given: more latitude for issuance decisions, authority for AASI/SI, opportunity to pursue "super AME" status, and authority to issue a temporary medical certificate given supporting documentation while awaiting an FAA decision (Table 37).

Table 37. Changes to decision processes/policies (count) from domestic AMEs

	Recommendation (22)	
Expand Authority (n=16)	- **AME (13)** [in general (6), (AASI (2), SI (2), AASI/SI (1), manage SI cases (1), depression screening (1)] - **senior AME (3)** [support Super AME program (2), certify statement of demonstrated ability (SODA) (1)]	
Issue Temporary Certificate (5) [awaiting deferral/AASI decision(2), with supporting info from A/M (1), in general (1), time limited for co-morbid conditions (1)]		
AME Input on Deferrals (1)		

Before moving to proposed changes for submissions of the examiner's report and supporting documentation to the FAA, needed improvements to standards and guidelines identified by domestic AMEs are presented.

Standards and Guidelines. Improvements were identified by domestic AMEs. They addressed the need for periodic review and revisions, in general, to clarify sections and reorganize the content so the process is easier to follow. Specific revisions would involve reviewing certification and SI criteria, bringing guidelines up-to-date and basing them on empirical evidence, as well as adjusting criteria for medical tests/screening and issuance. Detailed results are in Table 38, keeping in mind that standards for airman medical certification, in terms of acceptable medical tests and results, are dictated by law under Title 14 Code of Federal Regulations part 67; thus, standards are not easily or quickly modified.

The majority of recommendations (36 of 52, 69%) concerned medical test requirements and acceptable results. The remaining recommendations (16 of 52, 31%) concerned frequent and regular review/rewrite of the standards and guidelines as laid out in the AME Guide, to keep it current and to provide a clearer understanding of the AME decision making process within the context of the entire medical certification process.

Requirements for Class of Certification. Domestic AMEs joined the debate on 3rd class medical self-certification in their final recommendations. They showed support for both sides of the debate. Of the 15 recommendations, 9 were in favor of self-certification (1 with time of day and size of aircraft restrictions), 3 were not in favor of eliminating 3rd class certification requirement, and 1 was neutral in pointing out that with self-certification, the FAA needs to maintain surveillance of the airman's "adverse driving history." Three additional recommendations were made--two pertained to not precluding airmen whose medical certificate had been denied, revoked, or suspended, or authorization withdrawn from qualifying as a sport pilot, and one recommended elimination of student classification since the exam requirements are the same.

Table 38. Distribution of recommended improvements to standards and guidelines (count=52) from domestic AMEs

Bar chart (Percent): relax/expand 34.6; update 17.3; add 13.5; tighten 3.8; review 11.5; clarify 11.5; simplify 7.7

Required Tests/Results (36 recommendations)

relax/expand (18)	up-to-date (9)	add (7)	tighten (2)
- **extend certification to (10):** hypothyroidism (4), stable hypertension (2), stable thyroid disease (1), stable allergies (1), newly diagnosed diabetes treated with oral med (1), mild, short depression (1) - **remove as SI (5):** asymptomatic thyroid issues/ hypothyroidism (2), review others(2), sleep apnea (1) - **expand SSRI guidelines (1)** - **remove CSR for high BP (1)** - **extend reporting interval for pacemaker (1) to 1 year**	- use evidence-based criteria (5) - keep meds current (2) - standards and testing for color-vision deficiency (1) - BP requirements (1)	- **add requirements at 60 years and older (3)** – lipid profile, weight standard, treadmill test - **require OSA screening for any two of the following:** BMI>35 or neck circumference>17 or hypertension treated with 2 or more drugs (1) - **drug testing (1)** - **accept military ETOH screening (1)** - **add cholesterol test with high BP (1)**	- **BP criteria/ requirements (2)** – use JNC-7 guidelines - **replace ECG requirement (1)** with combination of identified risk factors, baseline treadmill test using Bruce protocol at age 40, and treadmill test every 5 years after 45

Content/Organization (16 recommendations)

review (6)	clarify (6)	simplify (4)
- routinely update(4) - validity of psych eval (1) - utilize AME input (1)	- **criteria/process for common diseases (3)**, e.g., second kidney stones, color vision, hypertension, CAD, diabetes, glaucoma - **SI determination policy (2)** - ensure FAQs are addressed (1)	- **difficult to follow entire process (3)** - **SSRI procedure (1)**

BP=blood pressure; CAD=coronary artery disease; CSR=cortisol secretion rate; ETOH=ethyl alcohol; JNC=Joint National Committee; OSA=obstructive sleep apnea

Printed Certificate. Recommendations focused on the need to reprint a certificate. Half of the four recommendations from the MFI group pertained to reprinting; one indicated corrections were needed. The domestic AMEs' recommendations are shown in Table 39. A related issue pertained to eliminating the need for typewriters, for one MFI AME it would mean allowing hand-written certificates. One suggestion, counter to eliminating typewriters, was to type the certificate and later enter the data and transmit the report. Two recommendations from domestic AMEs were to change the medical certificate, and one MFI AME recommended allowing student certificates to be printed.

Table 39. Changes to printed certificate processes/policies (count) from domestic AMEs

	Recommendation (9)	
Reprint Certificate (4)	- correct an error (4)	
Typed Certificate (3)	- type certificate before transmitting report (1) - eliminate need for typewriter (1) - use paper that accepts ink pen (1)	
Change Certificate* (2)	- add corrective lens restriction (1) - use "chip" on pilot certificate (1)	

*Another recommendation was to remove medical information from the front of authorization letter for SI.

AME Rules. Table 40 shows the distribution of recommended changes to rules governing AMEs from domestic AMEs. There were no recommendations from the MFI group. Half of the recommendations from the domestic AMEs addressed changes related to relaxing limitations on the number of locations, restrictions on staff in conducting the exam, restrictions regarding exams for family and self, and the requirement of 10 airman exams per year.

Table 40. Changes to AME rules (count) from domestic AMEs

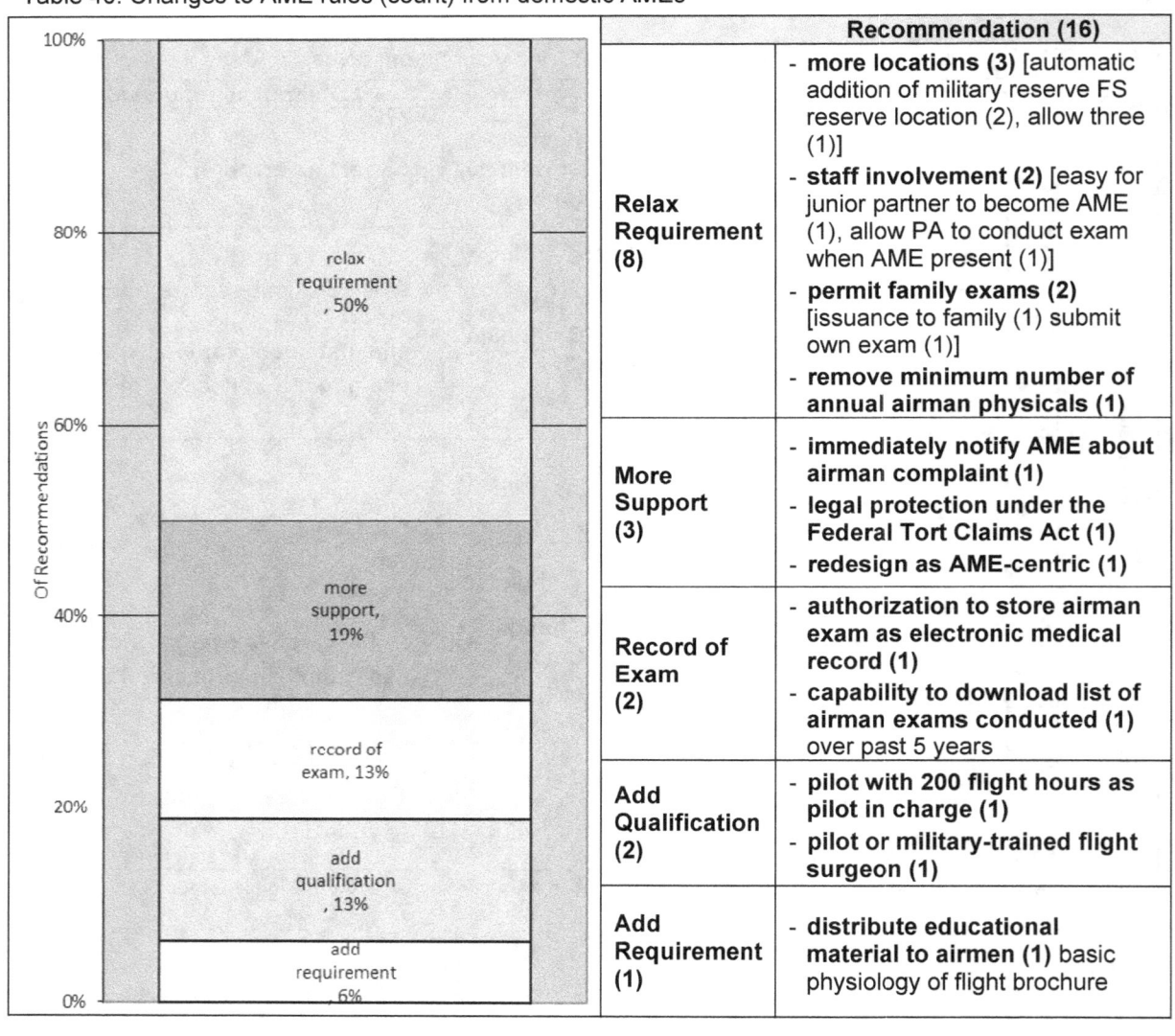

	Recommendation (16)
Relax Requirement (8)	- **more locations (3)** [automatic addition of military reserve FS reserve location (2), allow three (1)] - **staff involvement (2)** [easy for junior partner to become AME (1), allow PA to conduct exam when AME present (1)] - **permit family exams (2)** [issuance to family (1) submit own exam (1)] - **remove minimum number of annual airman physicals (1)**
More Support (3)	- **immediately notify AME about airman complaint (1)** - **legal protection under the Federal Tort Claims Act (1)** - **redesign as AME-centric (1)**
Record of Exam (2)	- **authorization to store airman exam as electronic medical record (1)** - **capability to download list of airman exams conducted (1)** over past 5 years
Add Qualification (2)	- **pilot with 200 flight hours as pilot in charge (1)** - **pilot or military-trained flight surgeon (1)**
Add Requirement (1)	- **distribute educational material to airmen (1)** basic physiology of flight brochure

Summary of Results for Changes to Medical Certification Processes/Policies. Table 41 summarizes results in terms of the top recommended improvements for each step of the medical certification process that the AME has a role in, and for changes to standards and guidelines, the deferral process, and requirements for class of certification.

3.4 Analysis of AME Comments Across the Service Areas

Responses that did meet the criteria for a recommendation were classified as comments and were sorted as negative, neutral, or positive. The neutral comment category included personal facts, questions, explanations, and hypothetical situations. The distributions of comments by group are shown in Figures 9 and 10. Overall, there were more positive comments than neutral or negative comments, although domestic AMEs provided comparable portions of positive (79) and negative (69) comments.

Table 41. Top recommendation for the medical certification process and AME rules

Airman Application (42)*	31% - make MedXPress optional 31% - modify items 17-19 on Form 8500-8 29% - allow airman access to previous application
Exam Appointment (36)	67% - allow AME access to applicant's past records
Standards and Guidelines (52)	35% - relax/expand standards
Issuance Decision (26)	69% - expand AME authority, with training
Deferral Tracking (6)	50% - use email
Printed Certificate (14)	46% - allow corrections and reprinting
Transmission to FAA (36)	56% - support electronic submission modes
Class of Certification Requirements (15)	60% - allow 3rd class self-certification
AME Rules (16)	50% - relax requirements

***(Total count)** is the sum of the number of recommendations from both groups; therefore, a greater contribution from the MFI group to the cumulative percent will result in a smaller count than the reverse.

4.0 DISCUSSION

Approximately one in five AMEs completing the 2012 AME Feedback Survey provided a written assessment of the quality and delivery of airman medical certification services during the 12 months prior to the survey by recommending where to focus program improvements. The service areas they assessed included the AMED, AMCD, RFS office, AMCS Internet system, MedXPress, ECG system, online information and publications, AME training, deferral process, and standards and guidelines for medical certification. CAMI used a content analysis technique to translate AME recommendations into actionable terms and to prioritize them. The majority of recommendations clustered into three areas for program improvement: developing organizational capabilities, enhancing systems/tools, and changing medical certification processes/policies. Recommendations from domestic and MFI AMEs were similarly distributed and addressed development of the human element of the program nearly twice as often as either system/tool enhancements or process/policy changes.

The higher-priority needs for developing organizational capabilities would involve enhancing knowledge and skills of program personnel and keeping those served by the program aware of requirements and critical information, so everyone is working together to attain program goals. By doing so, errors and rework are reduced, and effectiveness and efficiency are gained.

The higher-priority needs for enhancing systems/tools would produce gains in program performance with stable online access and user-friendly capabilities that support end users of the AMCS Internet system, MedXPress, ECG system, online AME guide, and OAM website in meeting certification requirements.

The higher-priority needs for changes to processes/policies would reduce applicant and AME errors and workload by providing airmen and their current AMEs access to past medical data/records. Resource use would also be reduced by transitioning to electronic transmission of all forms and supporting documentation.

Coupling the results from respondents' written assessments, which help identify issues/problems that interfere with AMEs performing their designated duties, with the quantitative survey results provides a better understanding of the level of FAA support that AMEs expect and potentially require as designees.

5.0 REFERENCES

Civil Aerospace Medical Institute (2012a). FAA aerospace medical certification services 2012 AME feedback survey comparison of 2010 and 2012 results: Domestic civilian AMEs overall. Oklahoma City, OK.

Civil Aerospace Medical Institute (2012b). FAA aerospace medical certification services 2012 AME feedback survey comparison of results: Military, federal, and international civilian AMEs versus domestic civilian AMEs overall. Oklahoma City, OK.

U.S. General Accounting Office (1996). Content analysis: A methodology for structuring and analyzing written material. GAO/PEMD-10.3.1. Washington, DC: Retrieved from http://archive.gao.gov/d48t13/138426.pdf

Graham, M., Milanowski, A., & Miller, J. (2012). Measuring and promoting inter-rater agreement of teacher and principal performance ratings. Washington, DC: Center for Educator Compensation Reform. Retrieved from http://cecr.ed.gov/pdfs/Inter_Rater.pdf

Stemler, S.E. (2004). A comparison of consensus, consistency, and measurement approaches to estimating interrater reliability. Practical Assessment, Research & Evaluation, 9(4). Retrieved from http://PAREonline.net/getvn.asp?v=9&n=4